FIVE CROOKS

AND A

KITTEN

Let's Try a Little

CREATIVE WRITING

Jay Lumb

First published April 2018
by jaylumbstories@gmail.com

Extended Edition published July 2018

ISBN: 978-1-5272-2340-0

Copyright: Jay Lumb

These stories and poems are the intellectual property of the author, Jay Lumb, and must not be altered or reproduced without the author's permission. Apart from my own family, most of the characters are invented.

Printed and bound in Great Britain by
CMP Digital Solutions

DEDICATION

Dedicated to all my fellow sufferers in creative writing classes. It's been a privilege to listen to your work and you have taught me a lot.

Many thanks to the group leaders, who produced so many interesting tasks for us to write about. What would we have done without them?

Keep up the good work.

If you enjoy reading this book, please send me an email at:

jaylumbstories@gmail.com

Novels by Jay Lumb

Book 1: Goodness Knows What!
Book 2: Goodness Knows How!
Book 3: Goodness Knows Where!

Cover: Jay Lumb

CONTENTS

What is Creative Writing?	8
Find Your Creative Writing Class	11
How to Improve Your Work	14
Show Not Tell	18
Five Crooks and a Kitten	20
Creative Poetry	26
Gerroff Me, Cat!	29
Workshop Tasks	31
Short Task: Creating a Mood	39
Pandora's Box: Contrasting Styles and Moods	42
Language Styles: Dialect, Jargon, Biblical	49
Limericks: Aeroplane Woes	65
Epic Poem: Raw Flying	69
Youngsters' Stories	74
The Old Lady Who Lived In A Vinegar Bottle	75
Who'd Be A Mum?	79
The Terrible Trios at St Loca's	82
Poem: Who Ate All The Pies?	87
Find Me Some Railings	88
Pity About These Nylons	91

Obsession	97
Spoiled Brat	101
The Adult World	105
Dorset Corsets	106
How Daft Can You Get?	109
Eel Pie Island	113
The Interpreter	118
Cash Flo	122
Poem: La Gioconda Mona Lisa	126
Poem: The Meek Shall Inherit The Earth	128
Unintended Consequences	130
It's That Man Again	130
The Interview	133
Poem: The Heathrow School of Sins	136
Howzat, Paul McKenna?	139
A Very Resourceful Woman	142
Hand Me the Valium – Innocent Accused.	145
Poem: The Monk	148
Selfless Devotion: Sheba	149
: Goodbye	153
Thirty Feet of Trouble	157
Puzz	162

Poems: I Miss the Sullen Skies, Wind, Rain	166
Workshop	169
Fantasy: Science Fiction	176
Poem: The Earth, our Home	177
The Butler	178
The Photograph	183
My Ideal Robot	186
Spoof Stories	190
Jesse Bond, Spoof Agent	191
What the Devil!	194
Spoof Poems: Geriatrica	196
The Critics: Ballet, Film, Books	200
Plays and Musicals	213
Radio Play: Arrest me, Please.	216
Workshops	222
Boat Stories	229
Idiots Afloat	230
Idiots Up The Creek	234
Idiots on the Move	239
Kelpie	244
Full Fathom Five	249
I Had A Dream	253

Out on the Scrapheap	256
Lost Love	259
Novels and Autobiographies	261
Preparing Work for the Printer	263
Shaping a Book Page	264
Handwritten Novels	265
Choosing a New Computer	266
Finding a Printing Company	268
Researching Your Family Tree	269
Illustrated Autobiographies	271
Narrative Autobiographies	273
First Chapters	274
Writing The Final Chapter	281
The Road Not Taken	282
The Stories of my Life	286
The Final Chapter	289
Creating a Book Cover	293
Final Jobs	294
Selling Your Work	294

WHAT IS CREATIVE WRITING?

Creative writing is using language as an art form, for entertainment, as opposed to conducting business, keeping records or conveying useful information. Novels, autobiographies, short stories, poems, and anything else that is entertaining rather than utilitarian is probably creative writing. The overlap is huge, of course. Think of newspapers, political pamphlets and advertising, all pretending to be factual but really trying to hoodwink us.

Creative writing is a demanding hobby, but a very enjoyable one, a fun way to exercise the brain: thinking up stories, searching for just the right word and for information in books and on the Internet. We learn new things almost every day. We couldn't learn so much by playing Bridge or Scrabble or watching TV game shows.

Many of us dream of creating a record of our lives for our descendants. We wont be there in the future, but maybe our thoughts and our words could live on. Imagine your own book on the bookshelf, a book as professional-looking as any in the bookshops. That dream is easier and cheaper to attain than you imagine,

What I cannot do is help you find a publisher who will give you a big advance and turn you into a best-selling author. Unless you are seriously famous, or have very helpful contacts in the publishing industry, you have about as much chance of achieving that as of winning a few millions in the lottery, but I can advise you how to get your work into print.

Many people claim to be writing a book. Few people actually finish one, and most of those texts stay just crumpled sheafs of paper that never meet a printing press. I've met one man who has written six thrillers, but they are still only hand-written. I expect they'll all go into the recycling bin when he dies. So sad!

By learning to be our own publisher, we can at least ensure that our works end up in a smart, convenient form that our descendants may be pleased to place in their bookshelves. It's hard to bin a book.

What do publishers do, then, if we need to learn to do their job? They find texts and people with the potential to sell thousands of books. They employ editors to go through the text with a fine tooth comb and change anything they don't like. They sometimes advise the authors to make changes, maybe to scrap their favourite chapters or change the endings or the titles. Then they pay printers to turn the texts into books. Finally they create publicity to persuade the bookshops to stock them. If the famous person cannot write a good book himself they commission a starving writer to interview him and 'ghost' write the book for him.

We're realists, aren't we? We don't delude ourselves that our fame or our work has the potential to sell thousands of books. We are delighted just to see our work looking as good as any book in the bookshops. That's why we don't need the services of a publisher. We only need a printing company. We know we are not going to make any money out of it, but it isn't going to cost us very much to give copies to all our friends and family. It's a hobby - much cheaper than golf.

What we do want is to be proud of our work. We aim to make it as interesting and well-written as possible. That's why we are reading this book.

We may still dream that one day our work will be read by a wider public, but one thing at a time. First, let's prove we can actually complete a book and get it into print. That in itself is a major triumph.

HOW CAN I USE THIS BOOK?

First I will make suggestions for improving your work; then you can see those suggestions put into practice.

My ten minute stories in this book were almost all written as homework for one of the four different creative writing classes I have attended in recent years. As an English teacher I used to teach creative writing, so why join a class? A class gives us an audience to read our stories to, and a chance to hear what other people can do when writing on the same subject. It provides a spur: the work must be ready for the class, or we will have to admit we have nothing to read to them today.

Sometimes the subject set doesn't appeal. We have to wrestle with it, brainstorm in spare moments for a day or two, until our unconscious minds at last drag something up from their murky depths. Then away we go, creating something interesting that we would never have thought to do, left to ourselves. It is those subjects that broaden our horizons, make us learn something new.

What if I can't go to a class? Well, you could recruit a few friends and neighbours to form your own class and use this as your text book. There should be enough material here to keep you going for about two years.

Not possible? Well, then, you can use this book to teach yourself. Before each story I have shown you the subject we were given to write about. You should write your own story before looking at mine. Then you can pretend that I'm your classmate and compare yours with mine: see what you can learn from the comparison.

Too much effort required? Well then, you can just read the stories for the fun of it. I hope they are entertaining. If you read them to a housebound friend it will give you something new to talk about together.

FIND YOUR CREATIVE WRITING CLASS

VERY SHORT COURSES

Many universities, training colleges and public schools run Summer Schools, offering one week courses, usually five half days, enough to give you a taste of the format and a chance to find out what would be expected of you. The internet is the best place to find them. Many schools are set in lovely countryside, offering a pleasant mini-holiday and a chance to meet interesting people. The tutor is likely to be a novelist or an experienced teacher. These courses are not cheap, and the students are usually good writers already.

The Guardian newspaper also advertises short courses in London, tutored by novelists or publishers.

ONE TERM OR ONE YEAR COURSES

Many local authorities and universities offer courses for mature students, often in the evenings. The local library should have details.

THE UNIVERSITY OF THE THIRD AGE

If you no longer work full time, the U3A is probably your best option. The U3A is a club, with branches all over the English-speaking world. Most towns in Britain have a branch of the U3A, often with over a thousand members, running more that a hundred free courses. For a small fee you can buy a year's membership which then entitles you to attend up to four different courses each week. The tutors are all unpaid volunteers, many of them retired teachers. Often there is more than one class available in your chosen subject, so you can try them all in turn to find out which suits you best. Most U3A classes are held during the day, between nine and four.

A TYPICAL CREATIVE WRITING CLASS

The size of the class depends on its length. There should be ten minutes available for each member of the class to read out his work, so a ninety minute lesson can accommodate eight or nine members - a cosy little group

The group leader will set tasks for the group to write and then read out to the class. Usually we write a story at home on alternate weeks, so we have lots of time to mull over possibilities, and maybe have a few false starts before the story takes shape. We aim for about a thousand words, which we can read aloud in about ten minutes. Such short stories are known as Flash Fiction.

We do not find fault with each others' work. The classes are not English lessons. We are experimenting with words and expressions, not trying to pass exams in the correct use of English. We all feel nervous about reading our work aloud to our classmates. If it is meant to be funny we are thrilled if people laugh. 'I enjoyed that' is a comment we all love to hear. Otherwise we just listen and put on interested faces. Who are we to dare to find fault with other people's efforts? Every book has its fans, but while some love it, others loathe it. One man's meat.

So, how do we learn? We write. We listen to each-other's efforts, including the group leader's. We evaluate them silently. We ask ourselves what makes that story interesting or moving. Why is this other story so dull and boring? Could we improve it? How? There is no need to say these things aloud and hurt anyone's feelings.

Sometimes members of the group will share useful ideas or a published author will pass on helpful tips.

Very few of us have completed novels. Some of us have started one. We all enjoy the feeling of having created something lasting, our short stories, instead of just whiling away our time watching TV or doing crosswords.

CORRECTIONS

Group leaders do not normally collect in the stories and return them covered in red ink. We are adults. We should take responsibility for correcting our own work, with a good dictionary to hand when we are writing. A word processor will flag up mistakes and suggest corrections. If in doubt I ask Google for examples of fashionable modern usage and spellings. American spellings are as acceptable as ours, so take your pick.

Often, particularly when we are writing dialogue, we might deliberately write in grammatically incorrect language to indicate that our character is not well-educated. He may be using dialect or fashionable jargon, or being jokey or boorish. Red-inking that would be most inappropriate.

Normally you read out your own work, so only you can see your spellings and handwriting. There is no need to type it, though it is good to practise your typing. You will certainly need to use a word processor for your novel, and maybe also for your autobiography.

WORKSHOPS

Every other week we have a 'workshop' when we must write something on the spot in about a quarter of an hour. The leader often brings in objects or pictures to inspire us. Many of us felt unnerved by this challenge at first, but we soon grew used to it. Now we just pick up a pen and scribble frantically. There's no time for second thoughts. The leader takes his turn to read his own work out to the group. One of the classes I attended was very quick to spot a joke, and we generally found plenty to laugh about. It was a fun way to pass an hour or so.

HOW TO IMPROVE YOUR WORK

SHAPING YOUR STORY

Films have taught us to expect modern stories to get straight to the interesting part with no dull introduction. James Bond films fling us straight into the action at a tense exciting point, even before the film title appears on the screen. We have no idea what is going on or why, but we can see that it's exciting and are eager for more.

So, we should fire the starting gun and get our story off to a flying start, with no prior description of the scenery or explanation of the historical background. Important information, such as who is running, where they are going and why can be dropped into the text as we run along. Endings too should be quite abrupt. When the interesting action has ended we don't want to stay on to watch the boring clearing up. Try to make your first and last sentences striking and memorable.

So much for the beginnings and endings but what about the middles? It's a good idea to watch a TV drama to note how the director has presented the scenes. One moment we are in a crashed car, the next in a market, then in a hospital and now in a kitchen. We are not usually shown how we got from one place to the other. We have to watch and listen carefully to make out why we are there and what is going on. We can use the same method in our stories: give the reader a little work to do.

In a one thousand word short story there is often no space for much description of the surroundings or the people. The action and the dialogue usually tell us all we want to know, - unless, of course, our story is mainly concerned with appearances or scenery.

CHARACTERS

The fewer individuals the better. Even in a novel it's hard to handle lots of characters successfully. The reader needs to remember where they fit into the story – and so does the writer. To make sense of some novels you need a cast list or family tree. Some have characters popping in and out all over the place, so it's hard to keep track of who is who and which villain did what and when. It's hard to care about any of them.

The most thrilling short story I've heard had only one character, a woman, trapped alone in a lift in a burning building. Only her thoughts and fears were described.

A crowd may be an essential part of the story, of course. Your character could be alone in a crowd or attacked by a gang.

Most authors write descriptions of their characters' appearance. Like a playwright, I prefer to leave that to the reader's imagination, for on stage many actors will play each role. As in a play, I want the language the characters use to reveal their personalities and feelings. If you enjoy writing descriptions you should do that.

We need to decide who is telling our story. Most authors 'play God'. They describe scenes and events with only God as witness. They take us right into the minds of most of the characters and describe their thoughts and emotions. The reader often knows more about their predicament than the characters do.

In my 'Goodness Knows' novels we see everything through the mind of one mildly autistic man. The other characters' minds and motives are a mystery to him and therefore to the reader as well.

In our short stories we can try out different approaches to see the advantages and pitfalls of each.

CHAPTERS

A thousand word story is usually written as one chapter. If you need to highlight breaks in the action - such as time passing or a change of location - you can leave a gap of an extra line to mark the break.

Books look forbiddingly dense and unreadable with no chapter breaks. I divide the action in my novels into about thirty coherent chunks and write each chunk like a short story. It's good to alternate chapters of high drama with something a little calmer if you can. You have to lower the heat if you want to be able to turn it up again.

I enjoy inventing names for my chapters, as a signal that I'm not taking the events of my black comedies at all seriously.

Chapter titles are seldom used by other authors.

LENGTH

Creative Writing classes prefer about one thousand words so everyone in the class has time to read out their work in one lesson. If your story is significantly longer it is wise to ask to read last, otherwise your classmates will start watching the clock, wondering if there will be any time left for their stories.

Magazine stories can be 1,000 to 7,500 words, a Novella: 10,000 to 70,000 words and a Novel: 70,000 upwards. Novels over 100,000 words cost more to print.

Very short stories include Flash Fiction: 1,000 words, Sudden Fiction: 750 words. Flash 500. The Drabble: 100 words. The Dribble: 50 words. Twitterature: 140 characters, and the Six Word Story:

'For sale, baby shoes. Never worn.'

LANGUAGE

We all remember school days when we were required to write formal essays, demonstrating our command of English and knowledge of the world. The language we used was business-like and formal. There were right and wrong ways of using our language: our work came back to us covered in red ink with a grade at the end.

Creative Writing is different. We are not writing purely to convey information or ideas: we are creating works of art with words. We are used to seeing paintings in a wide range of styles, from photographic to abstract shapes. Creative Writing is like that. It can be business-like and cold, or an incoherent outpouring of joy or hysteria. It can be polite and careful; it can be rude and boorish. Each of our characters should have his own voice, his style of expressing himself, and it will vary with his mood.

These stories and poems are written in a wide variety of different styles, contrived to fit the characters and the settings. You will notice bad grammar coming from characters who are either ill-bred, upset, distracted or lazy. Most people do not always speak in complete sentences and often say 'mmm' instead of 'yes.'

Writing 'experts' usually advise you to avoid cliches. A cliché is the most popular way of expressing a particular idea. Relaxed, confident people use them all the time, knowing their listeners are certain to understand their meaning fully and without effort. It seems perverse to avoid the best-known and most easily understood forms of language. However, if you dream of winning literary prizes for your refined prose you had better avoid them, and try to invent clever phrases no one has ever used before - but make sure your readers will be able to grasp your meaning.

SHOW NOT TELL

Writing experts will tell you to SHOW not TELL. What do they mean? You TELL a story but you SHOW a play. You can TELL others what you have seen or heard so they learn it second hand. When you SHOW them you perform the action in front of their eyes so they can experience it themselves, which is much more effective.

Most of my stories are written in the SHOW style. The characters carry on conversations in the way they would do in real life or in a play. You can manage with only one character if you make him talk to himself silently. Researchers have shown that 60% of us normally talk to ourselves silently most of the time. Literary critics call it 'Stream of Consciousness Writing,' and some authors are famous for using this device. See 'Pandora's Box 2,' 'I Love My New Baby' (Workshop task), 'Hand Me The Valium' and 'Pity About These Nylons.' It is a very effective way to bring an intensely felt situation to life.

Dialogue needs to be rather spare to be realistic. If you overhear people talking they don't usually tell the whole story or finish sentences: they leave their listeners to fill in the gaps. We have to tread a fine line (cliché) between sounding realistic and being unintelligible.

It is tempting to over-explain our characters, for example: 'He was a bumptious, overbearing man with a strong dislike of cats.' Don't write that: show us the man being bumptious and overbearing. Let's hear him in action, hear him being horrible to a cat. Don't spoil it then by telling the reader what he has just seen on your pages. That would be an insult to his intelligence. If you feel you have not pushed an important point home you could make another character react: 'You horrid man!

LET'S START WORK.

First I will give you the subject our group leader gave us when I wrote the story that follows.

Ideally write your own story before you read my effort. That is what you would do in a creative writing class. My story would be one of about seven stories you would hear read out by your classmates. You would listen intently and evaluate each of them silently. Is the story interesting, enjoyable, moving, amusing, boring? How has the writer achieved those effects? Does the language sound appropriate for that subject, for those characters and for that era?

None of the groups I have attended have criticised each other's work or tried to dissect it. Popular published work comes in every form imaginable. Different people like different stories. There is no right or wrong, just better or worse - in your opinion.

TASK: Write a story including these three things:

+ **an auctioneer,**

+ **a market stall**

+ **a cat with no tail.**

FIVE CROOKS AND A KITTEN

'Is this any good?

Gerald glanced at the necklace in Muriel's hand.

'Ah, yes! You can recognise a bit of quality, can't you? You really fleeced me last week, didn't you?' The stallholder was grinning his inane, ingratiating grin,

Gerald sighed. After only one previous visit to his stall, the man already had them tagged as serious buyers. Obviously now he would put up the prices of all this grubby tat. Well, he'd just have to bargain hard and get the prices down again, wouldn't he?

'Awtch!' laughed Muriel. A furry paw had appeared from nowhere and set the necklace swinging.

'Another blasted cat! Honestly, Muriel, you seem to conjure the damned things out of thin air. Just leave it alone. We don't want to be here all day.'

Muriel picked up another necklace to distract the cat and passed the first one to her husband.

Gerald shrugged. Might as well get out his jeweller's eyeglass, since he'd been rumbled. The sapphire was huge – well, something was huge, but it certainly wasn't a sapphire. 'Paste,' he said dismissively. The setting had a strange hallmark, but he'd seen similar ones before. 'Russian?' he asked. 'Know anything about this stuff?'

'Oh, yes. Very posh old lady, lived in the next street. Said she was a Russian countess. Called my wife in and gave her all this stuff last week. Must have had a premonition she was not long for this world.'

'Russian countesses, my friend, are ten a penny. Before the Revolution there were at least 150 princes, so Lord knows how many grand duchesses, etcetera,

etcetera. I bet pretty well everybody who wasn't a serf had a title of some sort, and countesses were right at the bottom of the hierarchy. This stuff, well, I might be able to move it on as scrap gold.'

'It's a very fine setting,' said the stallholder. 'You could get a proper sapphire put in. Would be worth a pretty penny, then.'

'I could use the man who took the sapphire out, if you could point me in his direction,' sneered Gerald. 'Does he keep a pawn shop, by any chance? That's an old trick, isn't it? The punter doesn't know enough about his own gems to realise he's not getting back what he pawned. Oh, put that kitten down, Muriel. You don't know where it's been.'

'Same place as the jewellery,' said the stallholder. 'Belonged to the countess. Now it's just a stray. Let you have it for a quid.'

"No!' said Gerald loudly. 'No more cats! They're absolutely lethal in an antique shop.'

'Look, Gerald. Look what the cat was sitting on.'

It was a large pink silk cushion with a heraldic device embroidered in silver grey.

'Isn't this the emblem of the old Russian Imperial State?'

'No use to me,' growled Gerald.

'No, look, all these bracelets, these rings and things.'

Gerald poked at the heap of treasures on the cushion with a sneer on his face.

'More scrap gold and a few bits of coloured glass! I could take them to the gold mart, I suppose. What do you want for them? Scrap, mind.'

'A thousand, the lot.' The stall-holder's embarrassed expression gave the game away.

'What! You think I was born yesterday? Think I know nothing about jewellery? I've been in this trade since I was knee high to a canary. Half that would be far too much. Let's go home, Muriel.'

'Seven-fifty's my rock bottom price, take it or leave it,' said the stallholder hurriedly. Now he had a truculent look. Time to compromise.

'I like the cushion,' said Muriel.

'Don't be daft, Muriel.'

'Alright then, five hundred. Five hundred for the lot, cushion and all.'

With a great show of reluctance, Gerald counted out a wad of grubby notes, then swept the loot from the cushion into Muriel's handbag. She winced at the weight.

As they sipped their coffee in the cafe just around the corner Gerald had a scowl on his face.

'What's the matter, Gerald? Are you thinking what I'm thinking?'

He leaned over and whispered into her ear. 'Get rid quick!'

'Mmm. I'd be - uneasy – if we put them in the window. The wrong people might just walk past and – sod's law.'

'Would be different if we had some provenance - '

'Maybe he could he get us something - '

'Pigs might fly! I could put a feeler out for Whingeing Willie. It's probably in his line.'

'We don't want the Old Bill nosing around again, do we? What about that little shop near Aunty Maud's? We could send her in with it. They'd probably give her far more than we paid, and still think they were swindling the poor old thing, wouldn't they?'

'Muriel, look at that notice behind you! There's an auction at Benson's tomorrow afternoon. What's the last time to hand stuff in for sale?'

Muriel turned to read the poster. 'Twelve noon today.'

'We could just make it. Too good a chance to miss.'

By four-thirty next day they were counting the spoils: nineteen hundred pounds profit, after buying and selling costs. Not a fortune, but not bad for a few hours' work. And what price peace of mind! The grave-robbers' loot was now burning holes in other people's pockets.

'Don't forget your cushion,' said the auctioneer. 'It was a good idea to display the jewellery on that. Very classy.'

'Thank you. I rather like it,' said Muriel, 'and the kitten.'

'That damned cat again!' wailed Gerald. 'What's it doing here? Thinks it owns the blasted cushion. Shove it off. You don't want a cushion covered in cat hairs.'

'Is this your kitten?' asked one of the customers. 'She's gorgeous. What do you call her?'

'No idea,' snapped Gerald. 'Belongs to the auctioneer.' Anything to distance Muriel from the wretched thing.

'Oh, you lovely little Princess!' crooned the woman.

'Prrt!' trilled the kitten, then jumped up onto her shoulder and draped itself around her neck like a collar.

'Princess!' smiled the woman, tickling its neck.

'Prrt?' said the kitten, staring up into her eyes.

'I've guessed your name, haven't I? Watch this everybody. Hello, Kitty! Hello, Tess! See? No reaction. Hello, Princess!'

'Prrt!' the kitten looked up at her with huge blue eyes.

'Have you had her long?' asked the woman.

'Well,' said the Auctioneer, unsure which way to jump, 'well, actually she used to belong to a Russian countess who died recently, so - '

'So you've hardly had time to bond with the poor little Princess.'

'Prrt!' said the kitten, then squirmed down into her cosy fur coat.

23

'Could you bear to part with the poor little thing? I could give her a very happy home. Would two hundred pounds be a fair price, do you think?'

'Well, I - -'

'Three hundred?'

Three hundred pounds for that weird little kitten, thought Gerald. It was a patchwork quilt of a cat, white with a ginger saddle, and black fur on its shoulders that looked like a foxtail cape. A black 'fox tail' covered one eye like a saucy feather. And the pathetic little thing had no tail. Must have got it caught in a door, or something.

The Auctioneer's mind was racing. How high would she go? Might she come to her senses and walk away?

'I think I could accept three hundred pounds, Madam,' he said, with a straight face. 'It's important that the poor little orphan should have a good home.'

The woman handed over her check and waved the receipt into Gerald's face.

'Look! Look!' she exulted. 'I've always wanted a Calico Cat, but they are so incredibly rare.'

Gerald read the receipt incredulously.

'One pedigree Manx Kitten. A fine example of a Calico Cat.'

'My own little Calico Princess,' crooned the woman.

The Kitten popped its head out of her coat. 'Prrt?'

1270 words

SHOW NOT TELL

The story above was written in the SHOW style.

Now let's see some of it in the TELL style – so much less effective, in my opinion.

FIVE CROOKS AND A KITTEN

It was such a bright morning it was a pleasure to get up early for a little bargain hunting. They soon got their reward. There, on the market stall, half hidden by the trashy bric-a-brac, Muriel spotted a striking necklace. She held it out to Gerald, the jewellery expert. Suddenly a furry paw appeared from behind a curtain of scarves and set the necklace swinging.

Gerald did not share his wife's affection for those little feline monsters. While she picked out another necklace to amuse the cat, he exploded with frustration.

To add to his annoyance he realised that the stall-holder had recognised them as previous customers. Was it Gerald's comb-over or Muriel's dyed red hair? It could not be their modest anoraks – most of the stallholders were wearing something similar. More likely it was Gerald's ferocious bargaining that had left a lasting impression. Hoping they had come to buy more of his trinkets the stallholder would surely put up the prices.

Gerald scowled and took a deep breath. Bargaining hard was his forte. He soon wore down the stall-holder's confidence in the pile of jewellery the cat had been sitting on. The coloured stones were only glass, he insisted, looking at them through his jeweller's eye-glass. Yes, the settings were genuine, but only worth the price of melted-down gold. The stallholder gave in and sold the collection of antique jewellery to Gerald for five hundred pounds.

As Gerald and Muriel savoured their coffee in a cafe nearby, the realisation dawned. It seemed most unlikely that a Russian countess had given all this valuable jewellery to the stall-holder's wife. It was more likely that they had now become receivers of stolen goods.

CREATIVE POETRY

Many people these days write poetry, but Creative Poetry writing groups seem hard to find. A few pubs occasionally hold 'open mike' nights devoted to new poets as a change from music makers.

Some towns have a poet laureate, who encourages events that give local poets a platform. Our town has a poetry bus, plastered with original poems inside and out.

There are a number of small competitions and arts festivals around the country that you could enter your poems for. Details are advertised on the Internet.

WHAT IS POETRY?

Poetry is language carefully arranged as a form of art. The sound of the words has a charm of its own, in addition to the meaning. It is the oldest form of story telling, its origins lost in the mists of time, long before writing was invented. For a long time prose was just written records of useful things like inventories and laws.

Story tellers, minstrels, moved from one settlement, one king's court to another, like pop stars on tour. They sang their tales of heroes and villains, love and betrayal in an exciting rhythm that set the audience's feet tapping. They built up a repertoire of poetic devices to enhance the sound of their performances: repetition of striking phrases or interesting ideas; sound games like rhyme and alliteration: these helped them memorise the stories.

Many modern poets have turned their backs on traditional poetic devices, so how can their work be described? An idea set out in an arresting arrangement of words? Something you can find in a poetry book?

HOW SHORT CAN A POEM BE?

'I think that I shall never see

A billboard lovely as a tree.

Perhaps, unless the billboards fall,

I'll never see a tree at all.'

This poem by Ogden Nash has everything a poem should have: rhythm, rhyme, repetition, humour and profound meaning: we are despoiling our beautiful world.

The very oldest poems are very long: very very long. The very oldest, maybe five thousand years old, is the Epic of Gilgamesh, the pre-historic hero king of Uruk in the Tigris-Euphrates delta. He was so big and powerful and exciting his people said he must be the son of God. (Most of the famous heroes of old were said to be the sons of God.) Because he was half mortal he was destined to die, so he set out on a search for immortality and the meaning of life. The best advice he could find was from an old lady inn-keeper: 'Eat, drink and be merry – for tomorrow we die.' He went home and built a city, to leave something of himself for posterity.

Rhythm, meter, can be a very powerful tool of poetry. The great prehistoric epics of Homer share a meter with the two thousand year old 'Aeneid' of Virgil:

Dah, diddy dah dah dah, diddy dah dah dah, diddy dah dah. Down in a deep dark ditch they are hiding waiting to kill you. It's the beat of the warriors' drums and the pounding feet of the armies.

The natural meter of the English Language is iambic, a limping rhythm going: di dah, di dah, di dah. That's why so many great poets have written so much in that meter, hundreds of plays and long poems.

They coul<u>dn</u>'t <u>help</u> it. <u>It</u> came <u>naturally</u>
Where <u>has</u> she <u>got</u> to <u>with</u> my <u>glass</u> of <u>beer</u>?
She's flirting with that chap with ginger hair.
You have a try. Too easy, isn't it?
Or would you rather have a mug of tea?

That's five lines of **iambic pentameter**: five iambs to a line.

My poem, 'Gerroff me, Cat!', is in strict iambic pentameter. It sounds like prose? So do most big English epics and plays – until you compare them with prose.

TASK: According to Google, the Guardian and Youtube, everybody is nuts about cats, so why not write a cat poem of your own, then have a look at mine. Alright, write a dog poem if you must.

GERROFF ME, CAT!

Gerroff me, Cat! Your claws are going through
My trouser-legs and right into my skin.
You're drawing blood, I bet, you little pest!
Gerroff my knees, I need a bit of peace.

What are you up to now, you crazy beast?
Come off those curtains - they're no climbing frame.
You'll have them off the pole. I can't climb up
To put them back, not with me gammy legs.

Don't turn your back on me and flick your tail
And sulk because I'm not much fun today.
Okay, I'm feeling grumpy - very true.
If you had half my problems, so would you.

You little monkey, off the sideboard! Aw!
My hearing aid's gone crashing to the floor.
I can't afford it mended, that's for sure.
That's it, you little monster, out you go!

Go terrorise the street till you calm down.
Go catch some vermin - just don't bring them home.
Okay, it's raining. It might cool you down.
And no use glaring through the window, Yellow Eyes!

It's getting very late, it's midnight now.
Where are you, Cat? Don't keep me up all night.
Puss, Puss, come in now, see what I've got here,
Liver and fish, your favourite juicy goo,
A freshly-opened tin - it costs the earth,
But then, you're worth it, as the adverts say.

It's cold here at the door, I'll catch my death.
Where are you, Pusscat? Hiding in the dark,
Tormenting me? Think I deserve a fright?
That monster dog has chased you up a tree?
You can't get down? I'll call the Fire Brigade.
Maybe that mangy fox has done you in.
Some crazy car has squashed you on the street.

Pusscat, come home! Don't leave me all alone.
How can I sleep without you on my bed.
Oh, Heaven help me if I find you're dead!

Published by Forward Poetry in an anthology called 'Perfect Pets'

WORKSHOPS

Every other week we must write something on the spot, without preparation or time to make plans. Give yourself fifteen or twenty minutes and see what you can do with each of the subjects I have had to tackle. Don't do them all at once. Alternate them with stories.

1. Continue a story.
2. Animals talking.
3. A Disastrous Present.
4. Advertise a vacant post.
5. Jealousy.
6 Create a Drabble.
7 Practise your punctuation

TIP FOR AVOIDING WRITER'S BLOCK

I often do a first draft on the backs of used sheets of paper. A nice new sheet, unused both sides, seems inhibiting, a dreadful waste of paper if I don't like what I've written. An exercise book can be even more inhibiting, if you feel completely deserted by inspiration. You may be putting a permanent blot in an otherwise nicely written collection of stories.

It seems much easier to write what might prove to be rubbish <u>on</u> rubbish. Then you can screw it up and aim it at the bin to get rid of your frustration. An office gives me stacks of waste A4 sheets, used on only one side.

15 MINUTE TASK: Continue this story.

Marjorie had noticed him staring at her all through the meeting. She felt distinctly uncomfortable. On the way home the fog started to thicken. She began to increase her pace. Suddenly she felt a hand on her shoulder - - -

It was happening: the nightmare she had foreseen so many times. It was all her own fault. She had always felt uneasy walking down this narrow alleyway behind the cinema. There were no lighted windows to run to. It was the perfect place for a psychotic killer to strike unseen. Her screams would be drowned by the roar of the air-conditioning machines and the hum of the high street traffic. She must be brave and fight for her life.

She took a deep breath and turned, her fingers curved into claws, ready to strike at his face.

'Caught you at last,' said the shadowy figure. 'My goodness, you do walk fast! You dropped this comb in the council chamber. I watched it slipping down through your hair. You were out of the door before I could pick it up. It looks like something special, Chinese or Japanese. Anyway, I thought you might be sorry to lose it.'

'Thank you,' she whispered weakly.

A bit of a damp squib? Surely you could do better. I hope you've had a try.

NEXT 20 MINUTE TASK: ANIMALS TALKING

LEAVE IT TO THE WOLVES

'Just look at this!' said the cook. 'I put these bones out at lunch time but the wolves didn't touch them. What's ailing them?'

"They're full, of course. Didn't you hear the noise last night?' said the housekeeper. 'Least said, Cook, soonest mended.' She bustled off out of the kitchen.

The wolves were warming themselves out by the boiler room grating. 'Here you are,' said Raoul, the big male, dragging a limb from behind the dustbins. The cubs locked onto it with their spiky little teeth.

'The flesh is best,' he said. 'That's why the humans usually eat it all. Make sure you don't miss any. Flesh tastes nasty after a few days.'

'There's a nice lump of rump here,' said Sheba, motioning to the cubs to join her. 'Save the bones till last. They don't go off.'

'Oh, look!' whined Raoul, 'there's more strangers coming up the drive. I'm stuffed. I can't eat any more, and there's no more space behind the bins. Let's move the remains of these up onto the mountain.'

'But what if these strangers are dangerous?' said Sheba. 'We shouldn't desert our post. Our humans are very kind to us. They save us all their bones.'

'Look, why don't we do as I say, move these up to a safe place, then come back and see if we're needed. We might have more appetite by then. If not there'll be room for them behind the bins.'

'You're the boss,' said Sheba. She sorted out the biggest, meatiest body parts for the cubs, locked her evil jaws into one of the skulls, then led the way at a gallop up into the mountains.   Word count: 275

NEXT TASK: Write about a disastrous present.

A DISASTROUS PRESENT

'And lastly, thank you all for your incredible generosity, for all these fabulous presents. We shall have great fun unwrapping them all when we get back.' The groom beamed at his smiling guests.

'Oh, but you must open this card now!' exclaimed his best friend, Joe. 'It wont keep till after your honeymoon.'

The groom took the envelope and pulled out a card.

Fantastic!' he gasped. 'A helicopter flight. At 5pm today! Can we make it in time?'

'No!' gasped the bride. 'We have to be at the airport at 7pm for our flight to Majorca.'

'No!' said Joe. 'You have to be at the airport at 4.45 This flight is only half an hour, so you'll have time for tea at the airport afterwards. I'll run you there. We'll call at your mother's so you can do a quick change and pick up your suitcases. The pilot's going to fly over the hotel while everyone's having tea so we can all wave to you.'

'Couldn't we wait till we get back from Majorca?' asked the bride. 'We'd enjoy it much more then, when we have plenty of time.'

'But that spoils all the fun for us,' moaned Joe. 'We want to watch and give you a great send off.'

At 5.15 the whirlie bird roared over the hotel. The guests laughed and shouted; the newly-weds waved.

The chopper soared up and away into the golden afternoon, up towards La Concha, Marbella's lovely mountain. Was it the sun, dazzling the pilot's eyes? Was it an unexpected gust of wind? Was it some devil seizing his chance to do something evil? If so he made a thorough job of it. The helo, full of fuel, hurled itself against the mountain. Nothing but ashes remained.

300 words

ADVERTS

1. Write an advert for a vacant post. Exchange adverts with a partner.
2. Write a letter of application for the job. Pass the paper back to the advertiser.
3. Write to the applicant offering the post or rejecting the application.

ADVERT

Wanted: Dogsbody for temperamental movie mogul. Must have a hide like a rhinoceros, be able to function on three hours sleep and concoct excuses for outrageous conduct. Pay intermittent but often substantial. Present Dogsbody retiring to a mansion in Bermuda. Apply to Herbie Wineston

APPLICATION

Dear Herbie

I've been a dogsbody all my life. I always do as I'm told. I try to get things right but people shout at me. It's water off a duck's back (is that like a rhinoceros?) I say it wasn't my fault, and blame other people. I don't know what intermittent means but it sounds a lot. Please, I need a job and I'd love to go to Bermuda.

Love, Jeremy Brown, aged twenty four and a half.

REPLY

Dear Jeremy,

I'm staying at the Ritz in Pall Mall. If you can get in past the doorman you're hired. My suite is 9a. If you are not outside my door at 9.15 tomorrow morning forget it.

Herbie Wineston

(Most of the class advertised for a carer for their mother. I decided to have fun with a boring task and my neighbour joined in the fun. We got a lot of laughs.)

20 MINUTE TASK: JEALOUSY

JEALOUSY

"Jealousy is an emotion I wont stoop to,' Eve said airily. 'A feeling much indulged in by poor souls who feel themselves slighted, passed over, ignored, inadequate; pathetic creatures who let others judge them, find them wanting, unattractive, lacking talent. Exhibit jealousy and you condemn yourself, accept their demeaning judgement. That's true, don't you agree?'

'I admire your strength of mind. I'd scratch his eyes out,' Janice huffed. 'After all you did for him! It's so unfair.'

'All's fair in love and war, as the sages say. One must rise above it all, float serenely over the tempest. Bless you, my children – and all that.' Eve examined the diamonds on her fingers and her long red nails, manicured to perfection.

'Just like a man,' said Janice, 'to go off chasing something young and fluffy.'

'He clearly needed a respite. I'm not exactly – fluffy.' Eve gave a sardonic smile. 'Too much haute cuisine must feel overwhelming to a man like that. And his intellect is not exactly Mensa standard. I had hoped to educate him, but, sadly, one has to accept that every man has his limits. He obviously realised that he lacked the capacity to equal my expectations. At least I managed to improve his dress sense. He now knows how to choose a good suit, though I still had to vet his choice of neck-tie.'

'He was back in cargo pants and a scruffy grey vest yesterday. I saw him filling up that old jalopy he's driving around in now. *She* must have very low standards.'

Eve sighed. 'Well, one can only do one's best. If the material is sub-standard the finished product is bound to disappoint.'

'I've heard a rumour that he's been up to something quite nefarious, swindling old ladies, or something. Nobody seems to know any details, but it must be pretty nasty. They say his firm has given him the sack.'

'Well, I fear he may have a great deal of trouble finding another job anywhere in this vicinity. I expect that he – and his – floozie – will soon be leaving town. Oh what a shame!' Eve smirked over her shoulder, as she headed for the door.

370 word

CONTRASTING LANGUAGE STYLES

Did you notice the very different spoken styles of the two characters above? Eve, the prima donna, sounds like a hard, controlling, vain, pretentious show-off. Janice sounds down-to-earth and sympathetic.

There's no need to describe either of the women: their dialogue gives them away. You could imagine their appearance and what they might be wearing. Clothes and hairstyles may be temporary but character is not.

MINI TASK: Write a 100 word Drabble

'People are grumbling about the coffee charge,' she said sadly. 'Should we make it free again?'

'But you need the money,' I said. 'Charging's a good idea. Everybody can afford two pounds. It's hardly fair to expect millions of poor people to pay taxes to subsidise classical music when they never come to concerts. All music lovers who can afford tickets should support the orchestra.'

'I'm so glad you think that,' she said.   'We need a new grand piano. If you have a hundred and twenty-five thousand pounds to spare we'd be very glad to have it.'

100 words

PRACTISE YOUR PUNCTUATION (Verb)
PUNCTUATION *PRACTICE* (Noun)

'Listen!' I said.

'Mmm. What?'

'It's a nightingale, isn't it?'

'So?' His fingers pawed the screen as if his life depended on it.

'Nightingales are special. Everybody thinks so.'

'Well, everybody's an idiot. What use are birds anyway? Noisy dirty things.'

'What are you doing that's so important you can't - '

'Stop nudging me. I nearly got a whole row lined up.'

'No! You're not playing 'Candy Crush'! You great baby!'

'Listen, want a few teeth extracted, free of charge?'

'That's it. I'm off.'

'Get lost!'   86 words

CREATING A MOOD

To bring a story to life we must create the right kind of mood. Is it a happy story? How do we make it sound happy, not neutral or sad?

Houses can look welcoming and full of life, or grim and forbidding. People can look approachable and safe, or threatening and dangerous.

We need to be aware of the impact of clues we might have given the reader, and, of course, make sure the clues are pointing in the right direction.

TASK: Think of a scene you know well and describe it twice, in contrasting moods. first through the eyes of a defeated man, then a successful man.

HOMECOMING: 1

Way up above the giant cedars, the Great House languished, beautiful and silent as a mausoleum. He stood for a moment, gazing at the monogram on his fine wrought iron gates. Then, glowering at the vacant Manager's Lodge, he walked slowly in towards the Dairy. Outside his cottage, Luca, grim-faced, was forcing the last of his possessions into his battered old Fiat. His youngest child sat watching, motionless, on the swing,

On he trudged to the Dairy yard. It was freakishly clean and dry. It must be weeks since the cattle had gone to be slaughtered. The alpacas, no doubt, had doting new owners by now. Only a few goats, too fly to be captured, lurked around the deserted buildings, giving him puzzled looks. Heaven knows what had happened to the wolves!

'Your family promised us a home for life.' Luca was glowering at him coldly. 'We always did our best for you, you know.'

'I know,' he muttered quietly. 'I know that, and I'm sorry – very sorry.'

169 words

HOMECOMING: 2

He strode in through the monogrammed gates and shook his fist at the vacant manager's lodge. Never again, he vowed. On the village green three children shrieked and laughed. If they drove those swings much higher they would fling themselves right off. No, he mustn't interfere. They must learn these things for themselves.

Cattle ambled towards him from the dairy yard, relaxed and comfortable, now relieved of their milk. He could hear Gianni singing and the splash of the hose as he washed the cow clap down into the drain.

A sudden flurry told him the wolves were at it again, playing sheep dog with the poor squealing alpacas and the wicked little goats. It was business as usual.

He gazed up at the far blue peaks and drew a breath of sharp clean mountain air. There, above the dark cedars, bathed in golden morning light, the Great House waited for him, beautiful as ever.

'Welcome home, My Lord,' said old Roberto.

164 words

PANDORA'S BOX

HOMEWORK TASK: Write a story twice, to demonstrate the effects of different personalities on what is basically the same story. In one story the man should be an extrovert and in the other, an introvert.

PANDORA'S BOX: NUMBER 1

'I hope you had a pleasant stay, Sir,' said the receptionist, with a practised smile.

'No, as a matter of fact I didn't.,' Henry Fanshaw growled. 'The baby next door wittered and whined all night.'

'Oh, dear! I wish you had called Reception. We could have asked the guests to lower the sound on their TV sets. We had no babies in the hotel last night.'

'No babies - ? Are you sure?'

'Absolutely, Sir. And we never give families rooms on the Executive Floor. We know our business guests need peace and quiet.'

'Well, one of Life's little mysteries, then,' he sighed. No point in pursuing the matter, since they were determined to deny it. He checked his watch: plenty of time to get to Heathrow for the Air New Zealand flight.

One had to hand it to them: Air New Zealand managed to take the sting out of a hideously long flight, first to LA, then Hawaii, then Fiji and now, at last, there below was Auckland, looking as nondescript as ever. The flight attendants had a disturbingly matey attitude to their guests, even those in First Class. The stewardess bounced into the next seat, then seemed about to climb onto his knee as she tried to peer out of his window.

'Look down there, Sir. That house with the blue roof. It's mine, and I've got three whole days to enjoy it before we head off again. Can't wait.'

Nice people, New Zealanders, he thought. Pity there were so few of them - less than five million in a country the size of Britain. What a miserable, empty place it was, unless you were particularly partial to sheep. There were sixty million of them. He should get this stupid chore done with as soon as possible and hotfoot it back to civilisation.

Ridiculous idea, the whole thing. He'd been very tempted to refuse to make the journey. Who knows what might be in the stupid box! Sandra had been completely batty, a sort of New Age Flower Child, probably into drugs, certainly went in for strange little rituals – quite exciting at the start. He'd been bowled over by her at first. Her exuberance was so different from his straight-laced, buttoned up family. For a few giddy months he'd even considered going native and marrying her. Crazy idea! Thank goodness he'd come to his senses and gone home to run the family business! She'd sent cards for a while, asking when he was coming back, but all that petered out years ago. It must be forty years since he last saw her. She must have been only about sixty when she died. Odd that she'd left him something in her will.

When the lawyer telephoned he had refused to say what was in the box. He didn't know, he said, but since her will had disbursed only a small part of her estate it must be well worth the journey. No, he couldn't open it. The will stated very firmly that only Mr Henry Fanshaw himself was authorised to open it. He must be sent a first class plane ticket and vouchers for two weeks in any one of a chain of good hotels.

'What if I decline to make the journey?'

'I really don't know,' said the Lawyer. 'She was sure you would come. She refused to discuss alternatives.'

The lawyer was clearly very pleased to see him. He led him quickly to a side table on which stood a very fine chest of polished wood with a decorative brass lock.

'There is no need to open it here,' he said. 'If you will just sign this receipt you will be free to take it away and check its contents at leisure.'

'No, no, I've no use for the box. I'll just take the contents out and then you can dispose of the chest, if you would be so kind.'

He signed the receipt and the lawyer handed him the key.

'Right,' said Henry Fanshaw. 'Let's get this over with, shall we?'

The lock was rather stiff but he managed to turn the key at last and open the lid.

What was this, a lacy tablecloth? Had she left him a chest full of table linen? Had she collected this stuff when dreaming of a wedding, a sort of 'bottom drawer'? He lifted out the cloth. A doll? It was the weirdest doll he'd ever seen, with an ugly wizened yellow face. Was this some kind of Maori voodoo? What on earth did it mean? Had she dragged him half way round the world to leave him a nauseating voodoo fetish?

He took a deep breath and reached into the chest. Let's get this voodoo doll onto the table and see what is underneath it. As his hands gripped the doll its surface layer crumbled into dust. He was holding something hard and shiny that seemed to leer up at him. He dropped the doll into the box and shut the lid with a bang. Then he slumped onto a chair and gazed at the lawyer in silent shock.

'What is it?' asked the lawyer, staring at him in alarm.

'Look, just look,' whispered Henry Fanshaw.

The lawyer opened the lid cautiously and peered inside. Then he closed it carefully and made his way back to his desk, steadying himself on the furniture. He picked up his phone with a shaking hand.

'I think we must call the police,' he said quietly.

935 words

PANDORA'S BOX: NUMBER 2

Why on earth did I agree to go, I grumbled to myself as the plane touched down in the middle of the night. LA was far enough away to be a pain, but that was only the start: now there was the whole Pacific to cross.

'Can I get you something, Sir? Champagne? Bucks' Fizz, something nice from the menu?' The steward handed me the menu again. At least the service was good, if a little unorthodox. Air New Zealand staff had a refreshingly matey attitude to their customers, even in First Class. It was quite a small cabin on the upper deck. The other two passengers got out at Hawaii so I now had the cabin all to myself, along with two stewards who seemed determined to do something for me.

'No, honestly, I can't eat another thing at this time of night. Maybe a mug of warm milk might put me to sleep for a bit. Is anyone due to get on at Fiji, or do I have the place to myself right to the bitter end?'

'Five people are booked on the last leg, but we'll try to keep them quiet. You just lie down and let me tuck you in.' She fussed like a mother hen.

'Breakfast on the way, rise and shine.' She was still bouncing around like a cheerleader after a whole night on duty. 'Look, Sir, that house with the blue roof down there. It's mine. I'll be there by lunch time. I've three whole days off.' She all but climbed onto my knees pointing out of my window.

Was it jet lag or the flu? Either way I didn't feel full of beans as I trudged around Auckland, trying to walk it off. Ridiculous to come all this way on what was almost certainly a wild goose chase. Even dead she was still giving me grief. Yes, of course I could have refused to come, sent back the First Class plane tickets and the vouchers for two weeks in good hotels. You'd have come, wouldn't you? Most people would.

New Zealand may be a good imitation of a wet Sunday most days of the year; the first settlers may have cut down every blasted bit of rain forest they could find - - and hosed off all the top soil to get at the metals just under the surface - yes, vandalism on a huge scale, but if you shut your eyes to all that, it is a nice quiet place to drop out of the rat race for a couple of weeks. It's hard to get a rat race moving with less than five million people in a country the size of Great Britain. Don't forget the sheep. Who can forget the sheep of New Zealand? There's about sixty million of the woolly little beggars.

Auckland seemed just as dull as when I left it forty years before. Thank Goodness I left it! I've done pretty well back in Blighty, though I say it myself. Whatever Sandra's left me I can well do without, but still, when opportunity knocks, the brave walk right in – know what I mean? The lawyer left me gob-smacked when he rang to say she'd made me her chief beneficiary. Why on earth? Haven't set eyes on the woman for forty years. Yes, we were pretty close for a while, all of six months or so. Even bought her a cheap ring at a sheep fair. It was just a joke, of course. We both loved a joke. I can imagine her now, up on a cloud, laughing her crazy little head off. She was definitely crazy, one of those New Age Flower Children, getting stoned on LSD and dreaming up all kinds of new religions. The lawyer said he hadn't known her then. When he first met her she could pass for a normal, rational woman. Really? Mmm,

Back in the hotel I had an hour to waste. I flopped on the bed and read through the leaflets on the bedside table. I'd need something to do for the next two weeks.

'Visit Queenstown for a cruise on the MS Ernshaw. See the original Bungy Jump Bridge. Spend a night at the Dunedin Hotel, where every night is Burns' Night, piper, haggis, the lot. Go to Milford Sound, the wettest place on earth.' Why? 'Visit a sheep station, round up some sheep. Hear Lazy Larry singing about sheep, sheep sandwich included. Come to a banquet: eat one of our sheep, Sheepadrome: come watch our amazing performing sheep.' You must be joking!

The lawyer put on a show of being pleased to see me, but there was something furtive in his manner as he handed me the key to a battered old chest.

'Well, here goes,' I said, with an attempt at jocularity. I must admit a few butterflies were dive-bombing my stomach. 'I'm thinking of Pandora's Box,' I said. 'You know, when they opened the box all the diseases in the world came zooming out.'

'I can guarantee nothing will come flying out of that box.' He was having trouble keeping his face straight.

The lock seemed slack with use. It opened easily. What's all this? What a disappointment! Knowing Sandra I half expected a jack-in-a-box. Not even a moth flew out. Ledgers, papers, leaflets, a great jumble of paper, and computer memory sticks in labelled bags.

'Mrs Stevens said you had a sense of humour. She thought you might like something fun to do when you retire. She left you this business.' Solemnly the lawyer pulled out one of the leaflets.

'The world's one and only Sheepadrome. See our amazing performing sheep. Tickets 10 dollars.'

946 words

STRIKING LANGUAGE STYLES

+ Upper Class Dialect.   Upstairs Goes Downstairs.

+ Working Class dialect.   Flash Spooks.

+ Jargon.   Rubbish!

+ Biblical language.   A Flight of Angels.

DIALECTS

A dialect is a style of language and pronunciation used by people belonging to a social class or place of birth.

The speech of the Upper Classes before the Second World War sounds very strange and exaggerated to us now when we watch very old films. At the other end of the social scale, working-class people often spoke a language that others found unintelligible. Television is exposing listeners to the dialects of the well-educated and gradually ironing out the differences.

Upper Class life can be constrained by the constant presence of an audience. The warning: 'Not in front of the servants,' was one reason for the 'Stiff Upper Lip'. It was important not to lose the respect of those beneath you, so feelings had to be suppressed to preserve the appearance of confidence and effortless superiority.

The next story is set in Rome in 1901, before the advent of TV and Radio.

TASK: Write a story about Upstairs and Downstairs.

UPSTAIRS GOES DOWNSTAIRS AND VICE VERSA

'Ahee!' Crash! Clatter! Clatter! 'Ahee!'

'Good Heavens, Man! Do you have a riot in your house?' bellowed the Duke, putting down his glass. 'First, the King, now you and I.'

The Marquis rose, with an apologetic glance around the table. Every face registered alarm, and no wonder, he thought. It was only months since the assassination. A pointless act: they were now ruled by King Victor Emanuel instead of King Umberto. What did these anarchists think they had achieved? Well, they had certainly alarmed the aristocracy.

'Please excuse me, Your Grace, friends.'

'Be careful, Cesare,' called the Duchess, as he headed resolutely for the door.

'Roberto, please fill up the glasses. Luigi, more amuse gueules for everyone,' said Lucrezia calmly.

'Cold water, quickly!' the Marquis shouted, then he strode back into the dining room.

'Please forgive me,' he said. Then he seized two jugs of iced water from the sideboard, and hurried out again.

The woman's screams had subsided into moans and whimpers, but turned suddenly into shrieks.

'I'm sorry, my dear, but it's for your own good. Hold your breath.'

'Ahi! Ahi!'

'Be quiet, you silly girl. The Marquis is trying to help

you. It's only water.'

Good, thought Lucrezia. The Butler is at hand.

'Heidi, run upstairs to your rooms and fill a bath with cool water - tepid, not cold,' said the Marquis. 'We don't want to give poor Judy a chill to add to the scalds. She must soak herself in the bath until the pain goes away. Please make her warm drinks from time to time.'

'Well, it doesn't sound like a riot, thank Goodness,' said Lucrezia brightly. 'If you will excuse me for a moment I will take a peep. Then I can tell you what is happening.'

She was just in time to see her husband striding up the grand staircase with a bedraggled maid in his arms, dripping soup and water all over his best evening dress.

Noblesse oblige, she thought, and he was playing the part to perfection, as usual. Yet another housemaid would now be totally besotted by him. Hey ho!

'Now, Moretti,' she said, 'do tell me what on earth is going on.'

'I'm deeply ashamed, My Lady. It is truly unforgivable, and with his Grace and the Duchess to dinner as well. The girl leaves tomorrow, first thing. I am deeply sorry I engaged the silly creature. We will not tolerate such incompetence.'

'Am I right to assume that Judy tripped on the stairs and spilled the scalding soup all over herself?'

'You are right, My Lady, and what a disgusting mess she has made!' Slippery soup was oozing slowly down the steps towards the tureen, now upside down at the bottom of the basement staircase, and the walls were covered in splashes.

'That tureen is very large. I'm not surprised the poor little mite hadn't the strength to carry it up all these steps – and maybe it was burning her fingers. Why did you not instruct one of our big strong footmen to carry it?'

'But My Lady, it is the maids' job to carry the food upstairs. The footmen wait for it up here at the top.'

'Why?'

'I am told it has always been the practice, My Lady, for nearly two hundred years, ever since the House was built. I promise you I shall make sure the girl's replacement is strong enough to perform her duties.'

'Moretti, it occurs to me that it may be unwise to dismiss the poor creature. These activists could claim we are at fault to set her dangerous tasks beyond her abilities. They could argue that we have a duty, moral if not legal, to nurse her back to health, then give her more suitable tasks within her capabilities.'

'But My Lady, how would they find out about her?'

'Who knows whom to trust these days? There seem to be activists around every corner. This is a strange new age, this Twentieth Century. Everything is changing, and at a startling rate. Did you suspect, ten years ago, that by the end of the century we would have electricity and bathrooms? Maybe the time has come to reorganise our household – but not tonight: we have guests to feed. How quickly can the staircase be cleaned?'

'Perhaps half an hour to clean it, and then another half hour to let it dry. Or we could just put a door mat up here at the top for the servants to wipe their feet on.'

'No, no. No walking up slippery staircases. But our guests are hungry. What can we do? I have an idea. Please remind me when the servants have their dinner.'

'Five o'clock, My Lady.'

'So, you will not need the Servants' Hall until when?'

'Not until supper time, at ten o'clock, My Lady.'

'Please lay the servants' table as quickly as possible. I shall turn the tables on the revolutionaries. The aristocrats will invade the servants' quarters for dinner.'

'But My Lady, surely the guests – and the Duke and Duchess - cannot come down the slippery staircase - '

'I shall lead them out of the front door, down the steps, along the parterre, and into the Below Stairs entrance. It will be a great adventure. Then we shall end the evening in a civilised fashion. We shall go back upstairs for coffee and brandy and have a good laugh about our daring excursion. The Duke has a fine sense of humour, and he loves surprises.'

'But all the porcelain is up here. Do you wish me to have it carried down the stairs?'

'All our beautiful Sevres down a slippery staircase? No, no. We will have the crockery you normally use for the servants' dinner. You will surely be glad not to have to carry all the dishes up and down the stairs.'

The Duchess was sneakily peering out of the dining room door. Patience was not one of her virtues.

'My dear Lucrezia, how dashing the Marquis looked, carrying that sticky little maid up the staircase! Do you think he will be able to find the way to her bedroom?' she smirked.

'I'm sure he will,' murmured Lucrezia, with a smile the Duchess thought looked far too complaisant.

'Well,' said the Marquis, when they snuggled up in bed, 'that was a most unusual evening's entertainment. Is there no end to your ingenuity?'

'You enjoyed it, I hope.'

'The looks on the servants' faces! They were shocked to the core,' he laughed, 'and the Duke thought it was hilarious. It will be the talk of the town.'

'The Duke tells me that he has no Below Stairs in his hunting lodge, just a huge kitchen next to the dining room. He has little trolleys to wheel the food and china around. It cuts down the work so much he needs far fewer servants,' said Lucrezia.

'We could turn the Morning Room into a new kitchen, and we could have a trolley too.'

"Why sacrifice a useful room? Why not build a big new kitchen behind the entrance hall?'

'Brilliant idea! And we could have lots of modern machinery. Maybe then we could dispense with Luigi. He's growing more insubordinate every day.'

'The trolley would need to be a strong one. The children would certainly try riding on it. By the way, the Duchess thinks you're having an affair with poor Judy.'

'Then the Duchess is a very silly old lady.'

'Sh! Sh! She has big ears,' giggled the Marchioness.

1200 words

TASK: Write a story in working-class dialect.

FLASH SPOOKS

"Joan's comin tomorn," said mi mum. "A'll get a tin a salmon fa tea."

"Not eard a squeak outer er for munths," said mi dad. "She's sent a letter, as shi?"

"No," said Mum. "I jus know. Telepathy."

"You daft 'aypeth!" laughed mi dad. "Telepathy? Load a codswallop."

Mum grabbed a wet dishcloth and scored a direct hit.

We cheered em on. Great sport!

When Aunty Joan arrived for tea Dad just growled: "Coincidence. Or sumdy passed on t' message an she'll not admit it."

Dad was a total cynic. "Don't believe in owt a can't pick up an throw," he bragged.

"Elephants? Mount Everest?"

"Get out an play," he growled, retreating behind his newspaper.

Conversely, he loved ghost stories, did his best to frighten the daylights out of us with horrid tales of monsters, demons, vampires and zombies. And, of course, like most tough working-class kids, we got a kick out of showing we were unshockable, could laugh and jeer at whatever life threw at us, even wet dishcloths.

One gloomy morning in January, Dad got his comeuppance. At the end of a hard day's work he was still decidedly off colour when he slunk into the house.

"What's up wi you, luv?" asked my mother.

"Nawt!" he growled, picking at his tea with little enthusiasm.

"Tha's getten the sack?"

"Don't be daft."

My mother told us the truth at breakfast next morning. Unable to sleep, he'd finally told her the tale.

As he was crossing the street two figures materialised in the pre-dawn gloom. They were walking fast towards him. If he hadn't stepped back quickly they would have smacked right into him. They were in fancy dress, the woman in a long dress and the man sporting a top hat. He could tell from their faces that they didn't know he was there, blocking their way, even when he was only inches away from them. Shocked, he watched them walk briskly on, straight towards a wall of heavy stone blocks topped with iron railings. They didn't even slow down, just strode on straight through it, then carried on walking - in mid air. There was a drop of at least eight feet on the other side of the wall - but they obviously couldn't see that either.

For the next few days my arch-cynic father went a round-about route to the bus stop.

"Dad, can we walk yer tert bus stop? Ask 'em what it's like ter be a ghost."

"Wha, you lot? Up an out the door by alf pass six? Don't make me laugh,"

My mother was right, of course: we always overslept. We contented ourselves with teasing Dad about the resident ghosts he'd invented for us: Horace and Boris, lurking down in the gloomy cellar, and Hector and Sector going bump in the attic.

"Our ghosts could invite yer new uns fer tea - by telepathy.'

                502 words   (Flash 500)

JARGON

Like dialect, Jargon is a style of language used by a particular group of people with similar interests. Unlike dialect it is not usually very ancient or attached to a class or region. It is changing all the time to reflect new inventions or fashions. Teenagers invent jargon to keep their doings a secret from the older generation and to make the oldies feel old-fashioned.

In many occupations people use jargon to discus the concepts they work with. Often they are proud of the fact that they can understand terms that mystify other people who are not trained or interested in that occupation. In other words, it is sometimes a form of 'showing off,' but it can boomerang onto the user, making them look foolish, if they use the expressions incorrectly.

This next piece of writing is set at a dinner for a group of atomic physicists. Few readers would persevere for long with a style as incomprehensible as this. Some would not even get to the end of this short dialogue.

Obviously language like this is extreme and could only be used in a story in small quantities for special reasons.

Practising jargon should shake us free from reverting to the colourless English we were expected to use in school essays, and give us the courage to be as inventive and different as we can.

TASK: Write a brief story in jargon.

RUBBISH!

'In my humble opinion,' the Emeritus Professor opined in his querulous voice, perusing the diners over his pince nez, 'the epithet, 'singularity', is an obtuse misnomer.'

My neighbour nudged me and confided sotto voce, 'His acolytes wax lyrical about his soi-disant revelations on the Higgs Boson. In my humble opinion, that elusive particle too much resembles the Philosopher's Stone.'

'And,' I interjected, 'this mythical Dark Matter is simply risible, more phlogiston, more ether, don't you think? I fear the ancient alchemists still lurk amongst us.'

'He forfeited credibility when he posited Kanada of Gujarat as the author of the first scientific treatise,' my neighbour sneered. 'Has the charlatan never heard of Zosimos of Egypt?

'Could it be that a superfluity of supercollider quarks has bombarded his neurons?' I chuckled. 'His extra-cellular fluid could be awash with complex clusters of highly entangled Posner molecules.'

'And Pixie Dust in the synapses is about as explanatorily powerful as quantum coherence in the microtubules, as Churchland said in 1996. Nicely put, don't you agree?'

'You are, I'm sure, familiar with Mordehai Milgrom's theory of Modified Newtonian Dynamics?'

'Of course. In my humble opinion it is undeniable. It removes the necessity to invent a putative invisible, undetectable eighty per cent of the Universe, a theory so absurd that future ages will regard our self-appointed Dark Matter experts as seriously brain damaged.'

'Consciousness,' continued the quavery voice, 'is likely to be connected with the quantum actions of interconnected microtubules. Gravity, acting on quantum states, causes them to de-cohere, as we are all aware. Isotopes of mercury have non-zero nuclear spin and might very well de-cohere phosphorus nuclear spin if caught inside a Posner molecule.'

'Couldn't a bang on the head achieve a similar result?' I muttered.

'Could quantum cognition make sense of what is missing from our understanding of neuroscience?' continued the old man.

'You have to be joking,' I spluttered covertly.

'His perorations fail to retain my attention,' my neighbour chuckled. 'The complexity of his verbiage appears inversely proportional to the significance of the phenomena in question.'

'A veritable Black Hole?' I proffered. 'Unlimited erudition inexorably absorbed, yet barely a smidgen of even randomised garbage is ever extruded.'

'An effective postprandial soporific?' he ventured.

We both laughed. 370 words

+ + +

TASK: WRITE A STORY IN BIBLICAL LANGUAGE

The majestic style of the great King James' Bible has helped to shape the English language. Translated into English in 1611, it's the language of Shakespeare's London. (He lived until 1616.) No modern translation has such power to invade our minds and refuse to leave.

The following story may be amusing (I hope) but it's homage, not ridicule. It's a pleasure to tune in to the melody of that powerful language.

A FLIGHT OF ANGELS

There were travellers, lamenting by the swimming pool, for their great bird, the Zebra-striped Britannia, was too sick to fly. Then suddenly, on the third day, it came to pass that the Angels of the Bird were upon them, and the glory of their smiles lit up their faces.

'Fear not,' said the Angels, 'for our Zebra-striped Bird is well again, and lo, it is eager to fly. Gird thy loins and hi thee to the bird, and climb ye into its belly, every last one of you.'

But the Great Bird, now sorely laden with six score students seeking more erudition in the land of the Germani, strained its great heart and sinews to reach the Heavens above Nairobi.

'Oh woe!' saith my husband. 'My poor wife, the light of my life, is verily now inside that great suffering bird that ought to be denied a flying licence.'

'Fear not,' said a voice. 'My dear brother cured the Great Bird's ills. He would not be within it now if he feared it might fall down onto us like the wrath of God.'

The Great Bird headed bravely into the heart of the wilderness known to all Mankind as the Sahara.

'What mountain is that there below?' asked the wife, now in the Great Bird's head, chatting up the Angels.

'We will name it for you,' quoth the Archangel, and verily wrote her name on his map. 'Shall we shy away from the cloud here ahead or bravely fly right through it?'

'Tis only steam,' laughed the wife. 'Go ye through it.'

The Angels laughed as the cloud seized the Great Bird and shook it like a dice.

'Aooo!' wailed six score students. 'The Great Bird is verily stricken by the wrath of God.'

'Verily thou shalt avoid the rest of the clouds,' spake the foolish wife.

'Methinks thou art not from the land of the Germani' quoth the Archangel, 'but rather from our land of the Angels – and the Angles. How goest thou to the land of thy birth?'

'British Birdways verily will fly me home from Zurich. Here is the token for my journey.'

'We must take our poor ailing bird home to cure it of its ills,' quoth the Archangel. 'or verily it will soon fall like rain from the Heavens. Be our guest, fly with us, then thou canst turn thy magic BA token into shekels once again.'

The Great Bird flew down to the earth at Zurich and the six score students departed.

'Hast thou loaves and fishes for me?' asked the wife.

'We have nothing, not even manna from Heaven. Go ye into this great aviary where thou shalt find much sustenance, but return thou must within one hour for then the Great Bird will fly again.'

Replete now, the wife returned to the gate and showed the pass the Archangel had inscribed for her.

'Hi thee hence, woman. We know of no birdline called African Safari Birdways,' said the Pharisees.

The wife showed them her pass marked 'British Birdways'.

'There are no more British Birdways birds tonight,' said the Pharisees. 'Hi thee hence, woman.'

'Oh, woe is me!' wailed the wife, rending her clothes and tearing her hair. 'The great bird will verily fly away with my luggage, I know not where, and I will be left to weep alone in this foreign aviary.'

At last, a good Samaritan beheld her, seized her and thrust her out through a secret door. With great speed she ascended into the belly of the great Zebra-striped Bird. There were more Angels now, and no room in the Bird's head for the wife. She sat alone in the Bird's great belly. Then the Great Bird, full of nothing now save Angels and the wife, rocketed so joyously up into the Heavens that the wife almost fell right down unto its tail.

For two hours the wife pondered where the Great Bird might come to rest. Then it began to fly in circles.

'Mayday! Mayday! Mayday! wailed the Angel Choir. 'Light our path to salvation, we pray.'

But a great darkness had covered the earth. All the Angles (and the Angels) were resting from their daily toil.

Mayday! Mayday! Mayday! Hoorah! Praise be to God, who has lit our path to salvation.'

Down on the dark earth a golden path had suddenly appeared. Verily it was a great miracle. Down swooped the Bird and ran along the path to glory.

The Pharisees were waiting at the aviary. They seized all the Angels and marched them away.

'What is this great aviary?' the wife asked a Pharisee.

'Stansted Birdport,' said the Pharisee. 'The first Angles (and some Angels) arrive at six-thirty. If thou desirest, their coach will then convey thee to the great metropolis.'

And so it came to pass that the wife was left all alone in the black dark empty aviary for four whole hours. Even the shining golden path had disappeared.

'Yet I fear no evil,' said the foolish wife. 'I can cash my British Birdways ticket for £68. I am truly favoured among women.'

856 word

(£68 seemed a lot of money in 1966. My husband, on business, had a free First Class ticket for a proper airline, but his luggage went adrift at Heathrow, so I got home first. I've no idea what happened to those poor, good-natured Angels, or their battered old zebra-striped Britannia.)

LIMERICKS AND EPICS

Limericks are usually only five lines long, but they are so much fun that once you start writing them it's hard to stop – as you can see.

Epics are very long poems recounting great deeds by famous heroes. They generally involve a dangerous journey and a struggle against fearsome beasts or tyrants.

We're not heroes, but our problems seem epic at times, so why not write some mini-epics?

TASK: Write a limerick.

This limerick was published by Forward Poetry in their book of Limericks.

AEROPLANE WOES

You've packed and you're ready to go,
Full of hope, with your faces aglow.
Yes, you've checked all your gear
And have nothing to fear.
No suspicion you're heading for woe.

The take-off at quarter past six
Puts you in a bit of a fix:
Do you drive through the night,
With a driver who might
Fall asleep and drop you in a ditch?

A hotel at the airport? Oh, right?
Would you dare shut your eyes very tight?
You'll be out of the door
By a quarter to four -
You'd far better stay up all night.

The airport you thought that you knew
Is morphing into something new:
It's doubling in size
Right in front of your eyes.
It's a puzzle to find your way through.

And it's not for your benefit either:
It's to make sure you spend your last fiver
On more useless tat
To take and bring back -
And it wont fit in your suitcase either.

The body scan's fun for the staff:
It affords them a very good laugh
At Grandfather's truss
And Sharon's fake bust
And embarrassing things we all have.

Merry Hell's other people, they say.
On a plane there's no getting away
From drunk yobs, screaming babes
Loud women enraged.
You must suffer them all, come what may.

The pilot is sick of his crew,
The plane and the passengers too.
It gives him a kick
To make them all sick
By rocking the plane fro and to.

The stewards are bolshie as well;
They are giving the passengers hell,
Serving sickening food,
Being frightfully rude,
Then locking the toilets as well.

Mid Atlantic at two in the morn
You may wish you had never been born.
In a can flying high,
Seven miles up in the sky -
You have never felt quite so forlorn.

In a stack over Hearthrug you're found,
Going round like a merry-go-round.
Oh, please, give us a slot!
We would give quite a lot
At this moment to be on the ground.

Now the carousel goes round and round
But your luggage just cannot be found.
Is it still in L.A.,
Or in Mandalay?
It's the last straw that grinds us all down.

'Did you have a good flight?' your friends ask.
You really should take them to task.
They must know what it's like –
Do they all go by bike?
----- Yes, why don't we - - - !

Never again! - until the next time.
Happy flying!

TASK: Now write a mini-epic.

RAW FLYING

A dozen little planes sit silently,
Their white spats seeming rooted to the ground.
Four pilots under training, PUT's,
Sprawl sulkily in cockpits or on wings.
Another Ryanair comes coasting down.
A lumbering freighter drags itself aloft.
'Why wont the Tower let us fly? It's daft.
The visibility's not bad at all.
The big jets are all flying. Why can't we?'
The problem could be finding our way back.
Computers link the big jets to the ground
And guide them down through fog. They have no need
To see where they are going. Recently
An airport's landing system ceased to work.
A pilot in a panic crashed his jet -
Forgotten how to land it without help.
All pilots once have learned to fly like us:
Two minute seats, big ear- muffs to dull down
The deafening engine just above your lap,
Propeller whizzing inches from your face.
Our landing system is our brains and eyes,
Some dials, switches, plungers and a map.
A satnav? No. A compass? Yes, indeed.

A radio squawks. Instructors rouse themselves.
We're off, but can't go far away from home.
The Tower says a storm is on the way.
Four engines roar, four PUTs begin

A final round of checks, then one by one
I watch three future pilots roar away.
They'll never let me fly a Jumbo jet,
Not even with a cargo of dead sheep.
Well, I don't fret. I just refuse to do
Whatever boring task does not appeal.
Around above the airport they're to go,
Learning to stall the plane up in mid air,
Then hoping to regain control, not crash.
If my plane dares to do a stall on me -
I've read the textbook; I know what to do.
Right now I'm hankering for pastures new,
An unfamiliar runway with a caf,
A mug of tea, a piece of cake, and thou,
My brave instructor, co-conspirator.
'Salisbury's not far. We'll fly up there,' he says.
'I'll book a landing slot, and tell the school.
And you can call the Tower.' I radio:
'Bournemouth Tower. Good afternoon. This is
Golf Alpha Bravo Xray Kilo, heading to
Old Sarum. Requesting clearance for take-off.'
'Good afternoon, Xray Kilo. You're cleared
For immediate take-off, runway 26.
Standard Tarrant Rushton departure VFR.'
Brakes off, a little throttle and we're off.
The runway is conveniently close.
I place her white spats one each side the line.
'Full throttle now. Stay on the line,' he yells.
When will I learn to taxi? Oh, good grief!
She's heading for that hanger! Straighten up!
Last week some PUT completely lost control,

Veered off the runway right onto the grass.
At last the snaking stops, our wheels are off.
Once up aloft we pass the other three,
Circling, no doubt with bated breath, poor souls.
My instructor chuckles: 'It's more fun with you.
We go somewhere; we see a bit of life.'

I stare down at the landscape; I must try
To memorise the landmarks on the way:
The snaking river, Ringwood's shining lakes.
'Old Sarum, look, down there, the ancient mound!'
Grass runways normally are hard to see,
But not today. It's bordered by small planes.
I touch down, but the wind lifts us again.
We bounce along the runway to the caf.

The café's full to bursting. What's going on?
'Nothing,' they say. 'The Tower wont let us fly.
We came to parachute for charity.
No chance, the way the weather's turning now.
You came from Bournemouth? How will you get back?
Look at the wind strength and those threatening clouds.'
My instructor, back from signing in, looks grim.
'One more notch of wind and we'll be banned
From taking off, then we'll be stranded here.
Leave that tea, Hun, grab that cake and run!'
To take off into wind lifts you aloft.
A following wind's not good, but ups your speed.
The windsock makes us gulp. It's blowing hard,
Right angled to the runway. It's the worst.

I guess that my instructor would prefer
To organise his own demise, not leave
It to his ancient pupil, so I say
'Would you prefer to do this take-off now?'
'You bet!' he gasps. 'At least the runway's long
And there's no trees or buildings within reach.'
Poor Xray Kilo nearly scrapes her wing,
Careering full speed almost on her side.
Cake crumbs and turbulence, oh what a mess!
'Finish that cake, Hun, then you take control.
Look at that great black cloud just overhead.
Whatever happens don't fly into that.
Lost in a cloud you can't tell up from down.
Your life expectancy's two minutes then.'

Eyeing that cloud I keep her flying low,
Skim Salisbury's rooftops frighteningly close.
What's happened to the spire? It's lost among
The dark grey streamers hanging from the cloud,
Like tentacles of giant jellyfish;
Or flying through an underwater wood.

I haven't hit the spire. I'm clear of Salisbury.
I need to find the Ringwood Lakes, but how?
I'm near as dammit flying blind. The map -
Check out the compass course and double quick,
Before we've lost all sight of Salisbury.
We're flying under Visual Flight Rules.
Should find our way by peering at the ground.
Someday I'll fly on instruments alone,
Trusting the speedos, altimeter, compass, map.

I'm getting intermittent practice now.
The Ringwood Lakes. They're there, right on the nose,
Black shining patches. Where's the river now?
It snakes along its flood plain. Here it is.
Now, somewhere to the right, far over woods
And fields and scrub, somewhere our runway lurks
If we have set the compass course aright.
A streak of grey gleams under leaking clouds.
'Our runway?' 'Yes, it looks like home to me.
We've made it, Hun. You call the Tower now.'
'Good afternoon, Xray Kilo, You're cleared to land
Immediately on runway 26.'
'Wilco, and thanks!' Now, get her safely down.
Get ready for that patch of turbulence
Before the runway: shakes us like a dice.
'Now cut the speed, not too much or she'll stall,
And smash her wheels off dropping like a stone.
Gently does it - now, just lift her nose.
Don't let the ground knock the propeller off.'
Back on her chubby little wheels she lands,
And I must taxi once again, but now,
At this low speed, she's docile as a lamb.

The other PUTs, weak- kneed with stress,
And bored to screaming pitch with circling,
Are waiting in the office. 'Where've you been?'
'Storm chasing, and we've brought a great one back.
Why should the young have all the fun?' I grin.

(Iambic pentameter again; did you notice?)

YOUNGSTERS' STORIES

TASK: Write an old-fashioned children's story like the stories of the brothers Grimm. Most old stories attempt to frighten children into behaving themselves.

THE OLD LADY WHO LIVED IN A VINEGAR BOTTLE

Once upon a time, long before your Granny – even your Great, Great Granny was born, and in a far away place you've never heard of, there lived a very old lady. She was far too old. She was so old her children – and even her grand children - had all died, and so had her friends. She had no business to be so ridiculously old.

All the guests said it was cruel to make such a very old lady scrub the floors and wash the dishes, and sleep under the kitchen sink among the spiders. So, at last, they told her to pack her bags and go home.

'But I don't have a home,' she wailed.

'Well, you can't stay here,' they said. 'We need the space under the sink for the new skivvy.'

Well, the old lady tried living in the church doorway, but everybody complained, so the Vicar shouted, 'Be off, you shameless creature!'

Wherever she tried to sleep the stray dogs barked at her and tried to bite her, so she trudged out of the village into the woods. There she found a very strange thing - a huge bottle, with 'Sarcen's Vinegar' stamped on the side.

It's ridiculously big, she thought. How could people lift it to pour out the vinegar? It's so big I bet if I tried I could crawl right into it. So she did. And she could.

It was nice and warm inside the vinegar bottle. It was right up against a big rock that kept off the north wind and sheltered by a huge sweet chestnut tree. She soon gathered up enough sweet chestnuts to last all winter. Well, things could be worse, she thought, and soon they were. When winter came it was so cold that her teeth rattled. 'Poor me! Poor me!' she wailed. 'What have I done to deserve this? I've worked hard all my life.'

'Whatever is the matter?' asked a tinkly little voice.

'What a silly question!' gasped the old lady. 'You can see what is the matter. All the other old ladies have a cosy chair by the fireside in their children's cottages. All I have is this freezing cold vinegar bottle.'

'I don't feel the cold, so I don't really understand,' said the voice. 'Close your eyes and tell me exactly what you dream of. I will see if I can help you.'

'In my dreams I have a cosy little cottage. There's a settle I can sleep on and a little table and a rocking chair. There's a lovely fire spitting and crackling and a big cauldron of rabbit stew bubbling on the ledge in front of the firegrate. Oh, I can smell all the herbs – oh, if only - '

'Tinkle, tinkle, whoosh! said the voice. 'Now open your eyes. Is this what you want?'

The old lady opened her eyes and gasped. There, in front of her, was a tiny cottage. The door was open and golden firelight flickered around a cosy room. There was the settle, and - oh my Goodness! That must be a rabbit stew – and she was so hungry.

'Is this real? Can I go inside?' she gasped.

'It's yours,' said the voice. 'Enjoy!'

'You're wonderful. Who are you? How did you do this?' asked the old lady.

'I'm a fairy. Granting wishes is what I do. Are you happy now?

'Oh, yes, yes, thank you so much.'

'Then go inside, out of the cold. Goodbye.'

When she had finished all the stew the old lady went into the village to spend some of the money the fairy had put in a drawer. She bought some more rabbit and vegggies to make another stew.

'How are you going to cook it in your vinegar bottle?' scoffed the other old ladies.

So she told them all about her wonderful new cottage.

'What! Does that fairy expect you to sleep on the settle? And you have to cook your stew on the living room fire? She's a very stingy fairy. Ask her for a proper house, with a kitchen and a bedroom,' they guffawed.

It was a few weeks before the fairy spoke to her again.

'How am I enjoying my house? Well, it's fine as far as it goes, but the other old ladies say you could have given me a bedroom and a kitchen – and a bathroom.'

'Oh, really?' said the fairy. 'Maybe I have been rather thoughtless. I don't really understand humans. Close your eyes and picture what you want. Tinkle, tinkle whoosh! Will this do?'

'Oh! Oh! Oh!' gasped the old lady. There stood a house, not a cottage, with four bedrooms, two bathrooms a kitchen, scullery - - everything.

When she tottered into the village to tell the other old ladies, they seemed shocked.

'You shouldn't have to walk to the village at your age. That thoughtless fairy should give you a horse.'

'I couldn't climb up on a horse.'

'No, she should give you a carriage, and a coachman,' they guffawed.

'After a few weeks the fairy came to ask what she thought of the new house.

'Well,' said the old lady, 'This big house is quite a chore to run. The maids are bone lazy, and the House-keeper thinks she owns the place. It's a problem to keep the servants in order without a butler. And the money you keep putting in my drawer is almost gone by the end of each month. I'm losing sleep worrying about the horses getting too skittish and turning the carriage over. And the other ladies say my new clothes are old-fashioned.'

'Oh dear!' said the fairy. 'I really must fix that. Shut your eyes and imagine all your problems going away.'

'Tinkle! Tinkle! Whoosh! 'Now, I promise not to meddle in your affairs any more. Goodbye.'

The old lady opened her eyes. 'Where am I? Which is the way home? Where is my house?' Then she saw the vinegar bottle, all alone under the chestnut tree.

She rushed into the village to tell everybody and ask if they knew where to find the fairy.

'Fairy! Fairy! You silly old bat. Only tiny tots believe in fairies. Stop telling such daft stories. Everyone will think you're demented.'

'Or possessed by the Devil,' said the Vicar. 'Be off, you old witch, or we'll strap you in the ducking stool. See if a dunking in cold pond water will bring you to your senses.'

The old lady tottered back into the woods and crawled into her vinegar bottle. Am I really going crazy, she wondered. My eyesight is pretty bad but isn't there a big square mark on the ground just over there, as if there was a house there, once upon a time?   1127 words

TASK: Write a story about a harassed Mum.

WHO'D BE A MUM?

What was that? Sally's brain floundered about trying to make sense of things. It was so hard. She was so tired. The clock, the clock, what time was it? Six something, six forty six. Why was she awake at six forty six? Something must have disturbed her. Listen, listen, concentrate. Whatever it was it must have stopped. Nothing but the faint whir of traffic on the main road. Listen, list -

Seven fifty three. Good. She had managed another hour of sleep. Maybe she would feel less harassed today. She'd always needed lots of sleep. Back home her mother had had to pull the quilt off her at ten on Saturday and Sunday mornings. Those were the days, gone forever. This new mattress was so comfortable. No, no, you can't do that. Get up, you lazy lump. The kids must be awake by now, wrecking their bedroom, as usual. Tea, you'd love some tea. And a biscuit. Tea, biscuits, tea. Get up, you lazy lump!

Rubbing the sleep out of her eyes, Sally staggered out onto the landing. The kids' door was wide open. Their quilts were on the floor.

'Jamie! Terry!' Nothing stirred. She picked up the quilts and threw them on the beds. None of their toys were lying about. What were they up to? She listened. Not a sound; only the distant traffic. The stairs. She had forgotten to fasten the gate at the top of the stairs. Oh my God! Had they fallen down the stairs?

She hurtled down the staircase and rushed from room to room. Nothing appeared to be out of place. - well, nothing more out of place than it was last night when she had staggered, exhausted, up to bed. Where on earth were they hiding? No trail of toys; no sound of movement. Sally scrambled back up the stairs, heart pounding.

'Jamie? Terry?' Bathroom, wardrobes, under the beds, including her own. Nothing, not even anything out of place. Downstairs again. Pantry, broom cupboard, behind the sofa. Nothing, nothing, nothing. They must have got outside somehow. Had they been kidnapped? Back door, front door, both locked, chains in place. Did the kidnappers come in through a window?

There was a stool against the sink unit. Who put that there? The window over the sink was shut, but not locked. Had the wind blown it shut? Had somebody climbed through that window, or was it a red herring? Surely she should have heard something. She had slept right through it.

You're a useless feckless mother, not fit to have kids. I know, I know. I'm too young to have kids. We should have waited till I learned more sense. Davey said the chance of getting pregnant was so low there was no need for contraception. He was doing his PHD in probability theory, so I was sure he knew what he was talking about. 'It can't happen twice,' he said. Ha! Ha!

Where are my kids? 'Jamie! Terry!' Please find me my kids. I'll be a brilliant mother, honestly I will, I will. They must be in the house somewhere.

She stormed around the house, searching everywhere again. Finally she opened the back door and ran out into the garden. Bushes? Shed? Garage? The back door to the garage was open. 'Jamie? Terry?' What's this on the car door. 'I LUV MUM'. 'Jamie?' Oh my God! White paint everywhere, over the car, over the floor, all over Jamie. 'Jamie, you little dope!'

I shouldn't have hugged the little villain. Now I've got white paint all over me. 'Where's Terry?'

Jamie pointed to the corner of the garage. There he

sat, surrounded by tins and bottles, eating something.

'Let Mummy have that, Terry.'

'Naah,' chuckled Terry, and held the big filthy pebble away from her.

'Let Mummy have a bite, just a little bite,' she pleaded.

He thrust it into her face. What on earth was it? Tiny teeth marks showed a few mouthfuls missing.

It was thick with soil and white inside. She sniffed it fearfully. A potato? A gift from the old folks next door who grew them as a hobby. Well, it may be filthy but it must be organic, she thought, on the verge of hysteria. But had he laced it with a tasty sauce from one of the tins or bottles. She picked them up in turn and tried the lids. All were tightly shut, thank goodness, the anti-freeze, the insecticide, the drain cleaner.

Dare she hope no serious harm was done? Should she call the doctor, admit what a disgraceful mother she was? Might Social Services take her kids away - put them with sensible grown-ups who would never let them stray into such danger. What did the Mother's Circle always say? Watch and wait. Don't panic.

Watch and wait. Watch and wait. But waiting is a sneaky form of torture, no wrack needed - - -

827 words

TASK: Write a boarding school story

THE TERRIBLE TRIOS AT ST LOCA'S

'It must be the toad.'

'But how did they find out? Did you say - ?'

'Of course I didn't - but some sneak must have.'

'Shush!' whispered Leggy. 'The Weasel's listening.'

Miss Ponsonby adjusted her pince nez and glowered at them. 'Compose yourselves, Gels. The Headmistress will see you now.'

She opened the door to a large, imposing room, lined with mahogany shelves full of grand, leather-covered books. Sunlight poured through the mullioned widows, projecting onto the worn carpet the colourful heraldic shields of the heroes who once inhabited this ancient house.

'Come here, Gels,' boomed Miss Arbuthnot, from the far side of her enormous desk.

Squinting into the sun, the three girls slunk nearer.

'It wasn't us,' croaked Binky,

The other two jabbed her painfully in the ribs.

'Shuttup!' whispered Freddo.

'Now, Gels, I am told by your house mistress - '

'I knew it,' hissed Leggy. 'She's shopped us – and she promised - '

'That you can be relied on to take care of a fellow pupil in distress.'

Staggered would be an understatement. The three miscreants gazed at her open-mouthed, then eyed each other warily. There must be a catch.

'A new gel is joining us today. She has recently suffered the most dreadful experiences and needs to be comforted and nurtured. Miss Jellico suggests that you are just the gels to shoulder this responsibility. Florabunda is only ten, two years younger than you, but she understands English fairly well. I am going to trust you gels to take the little one under your wings. I want you to ensure that she is protected from any bullying by less responsible gels. You may go now.'

Florabunda, all fair ringlets, was infuriatingly pretty. Her cornflower-blue eyes looked pink and ringed with dark smudges. She smiled a brave little smile and stretched a hand towards them.

'Why have you been crying, Florabunda?' demanded Leggy.

'I'm afraid they may be hurting my family. I think they may have shut them up in prison.'

'What did they do wrong?' asked Binky. 'Rob a bank?'

'I don't know,' she whispered. 'These rough men broke our door down in the middle of the night. Mama pushed me into the wardrobe. When everything went quiet my governess pulled me out. They pushed me into a car boot and after that I came to England on a plane. I have to stay here and hide until things are sorted out.'

'What a jolly great adventure! I thought people always suffocated in car boots. Weren't you scared you'd be dead when they got you out? Sounds quite exciting.'

Florabunda began to shake and turn a strange colour. She ran out of the dorm and locked herself in the loo.

'What a droopy little dope!' said Freddo. 'If her Papa is a criminal she'll be in for a life of crime. She'll have to toughen up, won't she? We should help her.'

'My parents say I shouldn't mix with foreigners and jailbirds. If Daddy hears about this he'll complain to The Snot,' said Leggy.

'Well, don't tell him then,' said Binky. 'Problem solved.'

Toughening up Florabunda was not easy. For starters she bruised far too easily. After a few games lessons she was black and blue from 'accidental' collisions with the terrible trio and blows from their hockey sticks. When they pushed her, fully clothed, under the cold showers or shoved her face-first into the loos she screamed so loudly the matron intervened.

She proved quite good at 'Fetch.' When Freddo lofted a ball over the high wall of the kitchen garden, Florabunda went straight in and retrieved it from the asparagus patch in no time at all. The gardener chased her out, swearing retribution.

'Why were you breaking bounds?' growled The Snot.

'I was the fetcher,' said Florabunda. 'Freddo threw the ball over the wall and it was my job to go and get it back.'

'Frederika!' boomed The Snot.

Back in the dormitory Freddo let fly. 'You nasty little snitch! You got me an extra hour of prep!'

'What did I do wrong?' asked the tearful Florabunda.

'Snitch! Snitch! Snitch!' yelled the terrible trio. 'You should never rat on your friends.' They grabbed their pillows and beat her to the floor.

If only they'd let me go to prison with my mother, thought Florabunda. It couldn't be much worse than this.

'Whoops!' breathed Leggy, as they headed out into the garden at break. 'Kayleigh and her scholarship trash.'

Kayleigh was no bigger than Leggy and co, but there was something very disturbing about the set of her jaw.

'Why don't you three take a running jump?' said Kayleigh, slowly and quietly.

'Let's go watch the hockey,' said Binky brightly. 'Come along, Florabunda.'

'Just you three. Leave us the little dolly.'

'But Miss Jellico said - ' began Freddo.

'F+++ the Jellicles! Scarper!' said Kayleigh, through clenched teeth. 'You stay, Pussy Cat.'

Florabunda still felt a little sick from Binky's last punch. She tensed herself, expecting the worst.

'Why d'ya cosy up to them nasty slags?' asked Kayleigh. 'They're just using you as a punchbag.'

'Miss Jellico asked them to look after me,' whispered Florabunda.

'Look after you? Look after you?' Kayleigh addressed the audience behind her. 'Didya hear that? The brain-dead Jellicles asked those trolls to look after this pathetic little kiddy.'

'I always said she was a sadist,' guffawed Jade .

'Sadist? She hasn't got the wit to be a sadist. She's a gold standard thicko,' laughed Bobby-Jo.

'I say we take over the baby-minding duties,' said Kayleigh. 'They wont let us have a pet, so this here's the next best thing. Pretty little Florabunda pussy cat. There, there.' She stroked Florabunda's soft golden hair.

Florabunda was too frightened to move a muscle.

'You're scaring the poor kid, Kayleigh.'

'Am I? Well, sorry, Kiddo. Only trying to be nice. Not much call for being nice in this hell hole, is there? You'll have to give me another chance. Now, do we want to give this poor little kitten a new home, Ladies?'

'Mmm.' 'Why not?' 'Poor kiddy.' 'Nothing else to play with.' The whole gang murmured approval.

'Right,' said Kayleigh. 'See here, Florabunda. Those three hyenas are notorious. Heaven knows why the stupid Snot let Jelly throw you right into the snake pit. Well, we're not going to stand around gawping any longer. You're moving in with us. We've a spare bed in our dorm. Once the vipers realise you're in our gang you'll be as safe as houses. How about that? I'll go tell the Jellicles, and the Snot.'

'Would they allow me - ?'

'Allow you? Don't make me laugh. They daren't refuse. We can put this place out of business double quick.'

'Really?' asked Florabunda, wide-eyed. 'How?'

'We're poor deserving orphans,' said Bobby-Jo. 'We passed loads of hard exams to win our scholarships. If they tried to chuck us out the Council would send an inspector to see what's what. He'd give this dump the thumbs down. All the paying parents would take their soppy kids away. This place would go bust in weeks.'

'We quite like living in this cosy old doss house. Better than a dirty slum in a city. Food could be better but the countryside's nice,' said Jade.

'We run rings round these daft teachers. They know far less than we do,' said Kayleigh, 'but who cares? As long as we've got Google and lots of good books we can teach ourselves pretty well anything. We'll teach you too. How about it, Kitten?'

Do I have a choice, wondered Florabunda.

She took a deep breath. 'Yes, please.'

1294 words

TASK: Write a poem in modern style about pre-teen children. (No rhymes or meter needed)

WHO ATE ALL THE PIES?

Who ate all the pies?
Why look at me?
Josh Walters ate far more,
Oh yes he did.
What? Joshy's skinny as a rake.
Well, lucky him!
He must have got a tapeworm
In his tum.
He charges round the playground
Playing drones.
He knocked me over yesterday,
He did!
I only ate one extra, honestly,
One more than Sophie.
And three more than Jill.
What's happened to your diet?
I don't care.
I'm going to be a model.
Yes I am.
A plus size model like Adele,
So there!

TASK: Write a teenage story about the Generation Gap.

FIND ME SOME RAILINGS

Norah Lennox glanced into the mirror on the hall stand, smoothed down a stray hair, and composed her face into a seductive smile. Then she opened the door with a flourish.

'Sophie! What are you doing here? Truanting again? Don't try to tell me it's another teacher-training day. You had one of them last week.'

'Aw, you don't seem very pleased to see me. Mum says you're always moaning I don't come see you often enough, so here I am. What do you want done, then?'

'Done? What do you mean, done?'

'Haven't you read the letter from the school?'

'What, they've expelled you at last? You've been asking for it long enough.'

'Naah! Course they've not expelled me. I'm a good girl now. Look, there's the letter on the hall stand. Haven't you read it?'

Nora picked up the letter and waved it in Sophie's face. 'It says here that Darrell Harmsworth has been allocated to me as a companion-help. Mrs Grant says it's part of her Civics course, bridging the gap between the generations. He should be here at any minute, so tell me what you want, double quick, then hop off, girly, and leave the coast clear for this Darrell Harmsworth.'

'Darrell Harmsworth isn't coming, Nanna. I talked Mrs Grant into letting me swop with him. Now I'll be able to tell Mom I'm coming to see you every week, and maybe she'll stop nagging at me. And it won't take up any of my spare time, so everybody's happy.'

'Are they?' growled Nora. 'What's he like, this Darrell

Harmsworth?'

'Alright,' said Sophie, with a faint blush and a wiggle.

'Oh, he's alright, is he? Well, then, why don't you get Mrs Grant to swop you back again? Then, if you ask me very nicely, I'll try and persuade him to stay on for tea and you can come as well. Then everybody really will be happy, won't they?'

'You'd rather have Darrell Harmsworth than me!' exploded Sophie.

I'd rather have almost anyone but you, Girly, thought Nora, but she kept that to herself. Maybe the girl was trying to turn over a new leaf. Pigs might fly! 'You'd rather have Darrell Harmsworth than me, wouldn't you? Don't deny it cos I won't believe you,' Nora laughed. She grabbed the girl and gave her a hug. 'Come in, child, anyway, and tell me all about him. Come and make me a cup of tea. Then you can tell Mrs Grant that you've done something useful. One teabag will make two cups. Look, I'll show you.'

'I'll have to do something else as well, or Mrs Grant will really give me grief. She'll think I'm just skiving off. I could go shopping - '

'Last time you did that you spent half my pension on eyeliner,' Nora laughed. 'No thanks. I enjoy shopping. Gets me out of the house.'

'Gardening?' Sophie raided the biscuit tin again.

'You must be joking! Last year's companion helps were a disaster in the garden. That idiot lad Mrs Grant sent to Myra Shepherd set her hedge on fire. Three fire engines came howling down the street – it was like a war zone. Myra's away with the fairies, so she enjoyed every minute of it, laughed her silly head off. But those other lads she sent to old Bert Entwhistle didn't get the joke. They met him at the door coming out in his coffin. They needed counselling when they got back to school. This Mrs Grant of yours seems a bit of an innocent abroad, lining up all this trouble for herself.'

'She's okay really, but you're right. She's got a lot to learn - and we're educating her,' grinned Sophie.

'Bet you are,' laughed Nora.

'I like those tights,' said Sophie, 'but aren't you going to put a skirt on? You'd have given Darrell Harmsworth a bit of a shock, answering the door dressed like that. He'd think you'd got dementia.'

'Tights? These are jeggings, girl. The latest thing. Look like tight jeans but pull on like tights. Get with it, Girlie.'

'Oldies don't wear jeggings. They're for teenagers.'

'Who says?' growled Nora. 'There's no law that says what old ladies have to wear. This is a free country. You wont find us oldies wearing burkas.'

'But you need the right figure to wear jeggings. They look daft on oldies.'

'Not half as daft as they do on most teenagers. Most teenagers are so fat these days they have legs like baby elephants. Look at that girl next door, bum like a rhino. Most oldies I know have far better legs than she has.'

Sophie sputtered with laughter and spilt her tea. Nora threw her the dishcloth. Sophie wiped up the tea and tossed the cloth back into the sink.

Rinse it out, you lazy creature! Nora didn't say.

'Have you read that poem by Jenny Joseph about old ladies?' asked Nora.

'Do you mean the one about wearing a red hat with a purple jumper?' asked Sophie. 'I'll be like her, some day, wearing purple and spitting.'

'And rattling a stick along the railings,' said Nora. 'I'm longing to do that, but I can't find any railings.'

'Well, there's a job for me,' exclaimed Sophie. 'I'll go find you some railings, then you can terrorise the street in your jeggings, like Gangsta Granny.'

' You do that. Girly, but what do we tell Mrs Grant?'

920 words

TASK: Write about a teenage crush.

PITY ABOUT THESE NYLONS

'Dear Sue, I'd love to meet you. Please come backstage after the show. Larry.'

I read it again – and again.

'Come this way,' said the usher, steering me away from the leaving crowd and through an unobtrusive door. The red plush décor of the Victorian Opera House gave way instantly to shabby plaster, but I barely noticed. This must be a dream: my little note had worked; he wanted to meet me. Now my dream had come true I wanted to run away and hide. What would I say? What might he expect? Surely somebody far more interesting than me.

Ahead a door was open and somebody was saying goodbye.

'Thrilling, as always, Darling. Give my love to Vivien.'

The woman pushed past me, then the usher nudged me forward.

I expected he'd be in a dressing gown, cleaning off his make-up in front of a mirror ringed with lights, but he wasn't. He hadn't shed a whisker of his stage persona. There he stood, feet apart, arms akimbo, staring at me quizzically, still every inch the great Roman commander, the over-confident lover of the Egyptian Queen. The Roman tan was only greasepaint numbers 5 and 9, but convincing, even from only two feet away.

And the costume – wow! The breastplate with the Roman eagle, the tough leather frock with the strips of skirt dotted with rows of bosses – all the metal gleamed like gold. The thick gold necklet and the armlets should have looked effeminate, but they enhanced his muscular build, while the Roman curls, fringing the strong square face, looked the epitome of masculinity.

What we talked about I don't remember. Maybe I was too overwhelmed to say anything at all.

I sat on the deserted platform at Manchester Piccadilly station in a daze. I'd missed my 10.50 train, but who cared? My idol had held my hands in his and gazed into my eyes. I had met the brightest star of the British stage and screen. I could die happy now, aged just 14.

When I rule the world all the men will have to wear Roman battle dress all the time. 'But won't their legs be cold in winter?' No, silly, they wore longjohns. 'Roman soldiers wearing longjohns! Don't be daft!' Who's daft. Look at Trajan's column. It's covered in Roman soldiers wearing longjohns.

And they'll all have to have beards. 'Romans didn't wear beards.' Well, Marcus Aurelius did, and Hadrian. 'And they'd all look like Karl Marks.' Well, they'd have to trim them properly, wouldn't they?

'Would Mark Antony have to grow a beard?' Look, I don't care tuppence about Mark Antony. Yes, he did a lot for Caesar, but Caesar did a damned sight more for him. And when the assassins did for Caesar, Mark Antony just went to pieces, straight back to the booze and gambling. Larry played him exactly right, I'd say. And then Octavian whopped him right and proper.

'Octavian, then. Will you make him grow a beard?'

Look, Augustus Octavian Caesar was God. I can't boss him around, can I?

'How can he be a god if he's a 'was?' He'd have to be an 'Is' surely.'

Look, according to ME, Octavian Augustus Caesar is just drop dead gorgeous, and a genius, so he can be anything he likes, so there!

At last it was 11.45 and my train was coming in. There was still no one else on the platform. I watched all the

92

passengers getting off. As I walked along the platform towards the engine I saw nothing but empty seats. I had a whole express train all to myself. What fun! I could have any seat I liked.

The engines always stopped close to the exit at Huddersfield station, so the front end of the train was best. My new adult shoes were pinching after a whole afternoon exploring Manchester and I had a two mile walk home from Huddersfield station. Best do more walking now, then rest my feet ready for the walk home. I chose the second carriage. I'd heard the first one always came off worst in a train crash.

As the guard blew his whistle four young men ran past my window swinging beer bottles and scrambled into the first carriage. Hey, this is my train. I didn't say you could get on. They were noisy, too. I could hear them fooling about. Eventually they appeared at the window in the door at the end of my carriage and started pulling faces at me. I tried not to look, but it didn't put them off. Soon they dragged open the door and gathered around me, poking fun at me and guffawing. I don't care what they wear they'll still be idiots, but beards would at least cover up half of their stupid leering faces.

The poking soon got embarrassingly personal.

'Look,' I said, 'I need the loo. You'll have to let me go or it will be all over you. I'll only be a few minutes.'

After a bit of a struggle I managed to pull free and hurried to the back of the carriage. I propped the loo door open with one foot to hide what I was doing and tried the handle of the door into the next carriage. It opened easily. Soon I'd put two carriages behind me. Then I got a shock. The blackness outside was like a mirror. I could see them - and they waved to me. The chase was on, Door after door I dragged open, but they were gaining on me. I began to run: so did they.

The door ahead had no window. I had reached the back end of the train. I looked around for the communications chord. If I pulled it would I get a big fine? And was there anyone near enough to be able come to my rescue anyway?

Suddenly the door flew open. A large hand grabbed the front of my clothing. It dragged me through the door and the lock clicked behind me. Now what?

'Well, that's spoiled your little game, hasn't it? Friends of yours, are they?' said the guard, with a funny look.

'No! Don't be daft! I'm trying to get away from them.'

'Oh, so, the driver's right, then, is he? Thinks you didn't get on the train together. Asked me to take a walk along the train. So, where are you planning to get off?'

'Huddersfield, but they say that's where they get off as well. Want to walk me home.'

'Do you want them to walk you home?'

'Not likely. Don't think walking's what they've got in mind, do you?'

'No, think you're right there, Love. Now, whatever are we going to do with you? Whereabouts do you live in Huddersfield?'

'About two miles from the main station.'

'Anywhere near Lockwood station?'

'Yes, just around the corner, but the expresses don't stop there, only a few slow trains.'

'Let's see what the driver thinks.' He clicked on the intercom.

'Lockwood, eh?' said the driver. 'Ask her if she can jump off a moving train.'

'Don't be daft!' I protested. 'The door would swing back and knock me under the train. I'm not that daft. I'm brilliant at jumping off buses, though, even if they're going really fast, but trains, well - '

'This door couldn't swing back and hit you, look,' said the guard, 'You could pretend it's a bus platform.'

I could see what he meant. It was a big wide sliding

door, as wide as a bus platform. It had to be so big so he could get all the big parcels in, didn't it?

'Listen here,' said the driver. 'I could slow right down as we go through Lockwood so you could jump off. What about that?'

'The station will be all locked up by now,' said the guard. 'You'd have to find your way out in the black dark, maybe climb over the fence. It's really high.'

'No problem. I've got eyes like a cat. But what if they jump off as well?'

'They'll have no idea what's happening. They wont be able to see you on the platform and if they tried to jump out the carriage doors would get them. They'd be in no state to run after you, would they?'

The driver was oh so clever. He didn't use the brakes, just cut the steam down silently so the train lost speed imperceptibly and the lads wouldn't notice.

The guard heaved open the big sliding door. He put one arm through a big handle beside the opening and beckoned to me. 'When I say 'go' just jump. No time to hesitate; the platform's very short.' With his free arm around my shoulder I watched the darkness roaring past like a whirlwind. 'I'll count to three - '

You don't jump out of a bus: you'd break your silly neck. You face the direction of travel, step calmly out sideways away from the vehicle, then run like Hell when you hit the ground, to shed momentum gradually. You'll know you got it right if you don't end up flat on your face.

It's only another bus, I told myself, staring into the roaring darkness. Was there really a platform there?

'One, two, three, go! ' yelled the guard, so I went.

My foot hit a solid surface, but those dratted fancy shoes nearly made me stumble. I slowed down as quick as I could so I didn't run right off the end of the invisible platform. I watched the train lights grow smaller and smaller, and heard the driver give me two hoots for good luck as he built up the speed again.

Then I stood very still, waiting for my night eyes to kick in and listening for movements. There was little traffic in the daytime in 1950, and none at all at night.

Why do unlit buildings seem so much creepier than the great outdoors? I felt my way to the ticket office, but the door was securely locked and the windows wouldn't budge. The fence was up on an embankment, so not so high as I first thought. There was a rockery – what luck! The topmost rock was right against the fence. I found another I could move and heaved it up on top. Standing on one toe I managed to get the other foot and both hands on the top of the fence. Wriggle, wriggle, pull, scramble. Last time I'll be able to wear these nylons.

The other side of the fence had no embankment. The ground looked a long way down as it came up to hit me. Aooch! I lay there in a heap, wallowing in self-pity for a few moments. Get up, you great weedy wet!. Can't stay here all night. The fence made a good substitute for a backbone as I struggled into a vertical position. Then I staggered to the end of the road.

'Don't you dare wake us up if you get back late,' my Mum had said. I looked at my watch in the light of the street lamp. One twenty. That must count as late. There were no lights in any of the terraced houses. I crept quietly along the street and turned my key in our lock as quietly as I could. Pity about these nylons!

1927 words

TASK: Write a story about a teenager obsessed by computers.

OBSESSION

'Put that down!'

'Wha?' He blinked and struggled to focus his eyes - and the absent brain behind them.

'Put that plate back on the table, that's what.'

'Hey, wha?'

'You're not taking that up to your room. I'm just not having it.' She seized the plate and plonked it on the table. 'Now, just you sit down and eat it here. Come on.'

'Wha the - ?'

'Look, a family is not a family if you don't even eat together. That's what everybody says. Now, come sit down and let's eat like a proper family.'

'Wha? A family? Just you and me?'

'Well, it's one step better than you upstairs and me down here all on my own. I spend ages making meals and you just grab the plate and make off up the stairs. I don't know why I bother.'

'Well, don't bother, then. I never asked you to. I'll just grab something from the fridge - or starve!' he snarled. He slammed the door, and she heard his footsteps deliberately thumping down hard on each stair.

Tears of frustration stung her eyes as she lifted her spoon and fork. And curry was his favourite meal. That was one of the very few things he had bothered to tell her in the last year or so.

She put her empty plate in the bottom of the sink and picked up his plate. What a waste! All that work. She couldn't just tip it in the bin. She dragged herself up the stairs and pushed open his bedroom door. What a sight! Bed a total tip, duvet on the floor, coke bottles, crisp packets, dirty underwear.

She put the plate down beside the computer screen.

'Eat it,' she said wearily. 'It's nearly cold.'

'Oh, thanks, Ma.'

'What? Was that a thank you? Well, that's better than a kick in the teeth. She would have to treasure that. It would be a long time before she heard those words again,

'That's a boring-looking game. I thought they were all big flying things racing around and aliens like Star Wars, and you had to shoot them all down with lasers and things, Pow! Pow!'

'No, this wouldn't interest you, Ma. It's just figures and stuff.' He tried to block her view, but she was having non of it. Well, from what she had seen, it didn't look like pornography. No heaving buttocks. Rows and rows of little white numbers on a black screen couldn't embarrass anyone, not even a teenage boy.

'Doesn't look a bit interesting to me. So, while I sit downstairs all on my lonesome you just stare at rows of figures. Honestly, Kyle, you really need to get out of the house, get some fresh air, make some friends. It's not good for you to sit here indoors all the time, no friends, no hobbies, no fresh air.'

'Look, Ma, I've got loads of friends. No problem.'

'Well, I've never seen any of these friends. You never leave the house. Why don't you stop truanting, do your homework and get some A levels? Then you could get a good job and stop wasting your time on all this rubbish. Think how good it would be to have your own money in your pockets.'

'Look, Ma! Just look at this.' He pulled out a wad of fifty pound notes. 'See? Now, look, just you go watch TV and let me make some more. Okay?'

'Oh, if you're so flush with money, how about a little -?'

'Look, Ma, take the lot. Now, leave me alone, will you?'

The screen flickered. He grabbed a pen and scribbled down a line of figures, then he turned his back and blanked her out.

Whatever was he doing, she wondered, as she clumped back down the stairs. Couldn't be shares and things like that. Surely he knew no more about business and finance than she did. Some sort of gambling?

There was somebody outside the front door. She could see the dark shape through the frosted glass. The bell rang as she reached the door.

Two men stood outside.

'No, thank you. I don't want anything today, and I don't do surveys.'

The men held up identity cards.

'CID,' said the smaller man. 'May we come in?'

Behind them she could see a white van with a strange antenna on the roof.

'I've paid my TV Licence,' she gasped. These men gave her the creeps. If only she had a proper man in her house.

'I'm sure you have, Mrs Moreton. That's not why we're here. We're visiting your son. May we?'

He pushed past her and set off up the stairs.

'He's not done anything wrong. He hardly ever goes out of the house,' she protested.

'We know that, Mrs Moreton. He's in his room right now.'

'How do you know that?' Outraged innocence gave her dutch courage. 'What right have you - ?'

'You'd like to see the search warrant?' He reached into his inner pocket and pulled out a sheet of paper.

It was a strange-looking form, but she managed to

make out the words 'permission to search the bedroom of Kyle Moreton - -

'Whatever for?', she wailed. 'What harm can he be doing in his bedroom, for Heaven's sake?'

'You've really no idea? Well, these teenagers are notoriously adept at keeping their parents in the dark, You son, Mrs Moreton, is part of a gang of hackers. They have successfully plundered the bank accounts of hundreds of thousands of innocent people. You will understand that we must take him in for questioning and impound his computer and all his records.

'As he is a minor, you have the right to be with him throughout the interrogation, along with the legal representative of your choice. I am required to warn you that anything you say - - '

980 words

* * * * *

**TASK: Write a story beginning:
'You never wanted anything good for me.'**

SPOILED BRAT

'You never wanted anything good for me!'

'Oh, that again!' sighed Lavinia. 'You don't need to shout, Aurora. I'm not totally deaf.' She sat back in her chair and stared wearily at her daughter. What was the charge this time?

'Why shouldn't I tell the world what a disgrace of a mother you've been to me? The public have a right to know that you're not the saint you pretend to be.'

'Saint? Well, that's a new one. I don't recall ever playing a saint, not even in a B movie. Now sinners, well, I thought I'd cornered the market in wicked ladies. They're such fun to act, and now I'm too old to play the young ones I can play the wicked stepmothers. Even more fun. Yes, go on, tell the world I'm a demon mother. Remind the producers I'm still around so there'll be even more good parts on offer.'

'You don't care, do you? That's the worst of it, you just don't care. You never did. I could sob my socks off and you didn't comfort me. What kind of a mother is that?'

'Crocodile tears! You're a chip off the old block, an actress through and through. You only screamed in a paddy when you couldn't get your own way.'

'You bullied me all the time. You said no, no, no to everything I cared about.'

'Let's think about that,' said Lavinia evenly. 'When you were about to dye the dog green I said no, I didn't think the dog would like that.'

'What the dog wanted was more important than what I wanted!'

'It's a mother's duty to set sensible rules to guide her immature children. No dying dogs is a sensible rule. Only a heartless idiot would want to dye a dog green.'

'So I'm a heartless idiot, am I?' yelled Aurora.

'Frankly, yes, my dear. I would gladly give you money to spend on mind-altering substances if I thought they might make you healthier and wiser – in fact I'd order you a ton - but I don't think anything you are thinking of is likely to do that, do you? So no, I wont give you any more money to buy heroin from that nefarious boyfriend of yours. I wish I could ban him as well.'

'Again, again, anything I want you always try to ban.'

'Ban? How can I ban anything now? You're grown up, nineteen, fully in charge of your own life. I have neither the right nor the duty to control you any more. What I want is neither here nor there. You can do as you like and you do. You always have. You never listened to any of my advice, in fact you went out of your way to do the opposite. You obviously enjoyed flouting me every step of the way. You were a perfect pain from the very beginning.'

'I take after you, don't I? And don't tell me it can't be in the genes because David is an angel.'

'I'm glad you said that. We can agree on something.'

'You see! You see! David's always been your favourite. You can't deny it. You can't, you can't.'

'Why should I try? David has always been a model son. He's kind, he's thoughtful, he's an absolute sweetie. You always treated him extremely badly. You hit him, you bullied him, you're eaten up with jealousy. You were from the moment he was born.'

'I have good reason. You always loved him most.'

'What did you ever do to try to make me love you? I had to lock my closet to stop you vandalising my clothes.

You pawned my jewellery to pay for drugs. Yes, you did. You pretended we'd been burgled, wasted lots of time for the police. Then the pawnbroker realised who you were and brought them back to me. I could have shopped you to the police and had you prosecuted for theft.'

'You should have given me a decent allowance. You drove me to it.'

'You always bragged you had a bigger allowance than any of your friends - until you met that bloodsucking boyfriend. He's just using you as a cash cow. Can't you see that?'

'That's nonsense. He loves me. No, don't try to tell me he's two-timing me. I don't believe that for a minute. You're just jealous because he's so good looking. It's not his fault if women hit on him all the time, is it?'

'Aurora, they're just desperate for the next fix – just like you. He's got you all on long lines, just enjoying himself playing with you all. However much you give him it won't be enough: he'll keep upping the price again and again. You're asking me to finance a drug pusher and I wont. No decent parent would. I should shop him to the police.'

'Don't you dare! You'll be sorry. I'll make sure of that. When everybody reads my book they'll know you're a monster and they wont believe anything you say against him. You'll just be doing what you've always done.'

'What I've always done is work my hide off providing a great home for my kids. Swimming pools, ponies, wardrobes full of clothes, parties for all your friends, however obnoxious. Lovely kind nannies, the best schools. And you behaved so badly the nannies threw in the towel and the schools threw you out for being cocky and disruptive. You're too idle to go to college and make an effort to qualify for anything useful. You just assume I'll leave you a big trust fund so you can idle your life away with your druggy friends. Well, you're in for a nasty shock. I have just set up a trust fund – to help the helpless poor and disadvantaged, not the undeserving rich. David encouraged me. He doesn't want any of my money. He wants to make his own way in life.'

'What? You've cut me out of your will? You can't do that, I'm your daughter. How will I pay all my debts?'

'I'll pay for a two year course in something useful. Let me know when you've been offered a place.'

'I'll make far more money from this tell-all book I'm writing. You'll be sorry.'

'I doubt if any publisher would print it. I'd certainly sue them for libel. I've got plenty of evidence in writing about your misdeeds, remember. And I'd offer them my autobiography instead. They've been clamouring for it for years. With my famous name on the cover it will sell like hot cakes.'

'What, you write a book! You're a dozy dyslexic. Can hardly spell your own name!'

'I don't need to be able to write. The publishers will find me a ghost writer. She'll record what I tell her and turn it into a book, a book about a demon daughter.

'And now, I'm afraid I'll have to turn you out. I've an interview to do for Vogue. And you're quite wrong: I do want good things for you. I want you clean, off the heroin and off that drug-pusher boyfriend. The trouble is you're hell-bent on your own destruction. There is nothing I can do,'

                                    1215 words

+ + +

THE ADULT WORLD

TASK: '**We have to write a story including the word 'Dorset',** I told my neighbour.

'Dorset Corsets,' he laughed.

'Thanks, I'll go with that,' I said, so I did.

DORSET CORSETS

"If we're going to get married we'll just have to get a job," Josh insisted. "We'll have to go to the careers office. I can't see any alternative."

I groaned. Things looked hopeless. We'd e-mailed every university and museum we could think of, but nobody expected to have any vacancies for experts in Ancient Egyptian or Assyrian hieroglyphics. It seemed we just had to get back into the real world of the Twenty First Century.

The careers officers gave us pitying looks when we showed them our PhDs. What a waste of seven years, they implied. Maybe we should take a course in something useful next to make ourselves employable.

"According to my mother," I said, "My Aunty Maud is desperate to get some help in her shop. We could see if she would take us on. Retail experience might make our C.Vs look a little better."

Selling corsets was not the way we had expected our lives to go, but our egos had taken a salutary beating. Beggars can't be choosers, so they say, and, to be honest, now I could read those intriguing-looking hieroglyphics I realised how excruciatingly boring they were. "Pharaoh is the greatest. He has ground his enemies into dust. May Pharaoh live forever in the lap of the Gods." Thrilling stuff!

The corsets themselves were quite a shock. Aunty

Maud didn't seem the least embarrassed by them. Well, old people often seem rather naïve, don't they, and she is eighty-one. They were not fashionable; would look quite odd under easy-to-wear modern clothes. They were mostly basques, designed to force the figure into a stiff S shape, emphasising the breast and bottom. There were red ones and black ones and a few white ones, all in shiny satin and stiffened with strips of something rigid.

"That's real whalebone," said Aunt Maud.

The people who came into Dorset Corsets had a furtive shifty look. They must be buying them for naughty sexy games or to pose for selfies for the Daily Mail 'Strip of Shame'.

Unfortunately the customers were too thin on the ground in this small Dorset town. The shop wasn't breaking even. If it were to close we would lose both our jobs and our home, for Aunt Maud had let us make a cosy home above the shop.

"Why not let us source some nice modern underwear that should be easier to sell?" asked Josh.

The modern body-shapers were nowhere near as pretty as the old-fashioned whale-boned basques. They were trying to be invisible in their creepy-looking flesh colour. It was not much fun helping overweight people struggle into the stretchy monstrosities, hoping to tame their unwanted curves.

"They give me the creeps," moaned Josh, "Like nasty big slugs."

"You horrid man!" I laughed, but I saw his point.

We continued to sell the Edwardian styled basques because they cheered us up, and looked so much nicer in the windows. I sewed bows on them, which seemed to improve the sales. Josh managed to get three Edwardian mannequins from the cellars of a derelict department store. We cleaned them up, bought them wigs and gave them gorgeous hairstyles with jewelled combs and flowers. Belles of the ball, they were.

"Time to let you into my secret, dears," said Aunty Maud. "Now you've learned how to run the shop I'm going to retire and hand it over to you. You can run it any way you like. All my friends are moving into that new block of sheltered flats and I'd like to join them. I've spotted a lovely flat."

To our amazement, when the legal documents arrived for signing, she had made over the whole of the building to us. We now had a large Georgian town house with big bow windows, three floors and a basement.

"Aunty Maud, you're amazing!" we gasped.

"Well, I can't take it where I'm going, can I?"

What a brave and jolly old soul she was!

"Good morning. Is this a museum?" asked a couple we had never seen before. "Love the ladies in the window. Just like the saloon girls you see in the old cowboy and Indian films."

I laughed and began to shake my head, but Josh intervened with a big grin.

"You're right," he said. "How clever of you to guess. We are going to open a museum very soon. We're just starting to get the exhibits together. It will be a museum of underwear through the ages, right back to the Egyptians and the Assyrians. Their ladies wore basques like these as well. We can make sure those exhibits are absolutely authentic: we are both experts in those eras."

"Are you going to keep the shop?" asked the woman. "Are these body shapers for sale. I could certainly use one of these right now. My nice new frock is showing too many bulges."

"Curves, Sweetheart," laughed the man. "And while she's trying those things on, can you find her a nice red basque as well? I'll buy her that for her birthday.'

900 words

TASK: Write a story about the folly of youth

HOW DAFT CAN YOU GET?

In the Autumn of 1956 Mike volunteered to run the bureau arranging casual work for hard-up students. Altruistic? No. He got a nice little office from where he could watch the girls coming in and out of the Students' Union building, plus first pick of all the best jobs. And it passed the time while he waited for his application for PHD funding to be approved.

Suddenly the office was full of bewildered and desperate Egyptian students, begging for work. Overnight they had become enemy aliens, with all their funds frozen. Our Government, in cahoots with our traditional worst enemy, had declared war on their country, just because they had nationalised their canal. NO! Yes, really. To pay for the war, funding for higher degrees was axed. Mike was ordered to report for deferred National Service.

'I've been thinking,' he said. 'If we get married now and I get killed you'll be a war widow. They'll give you a pension for life, so you'll never starve.' You think about things like that when you're poor.

How sweet! If he'd tried the usual - sign up for life as my unpaid drudge and sex slave - I'd have told him to take a running jump, even though he looked like David Beckham and could actually talk. And he had a great sense of humour. But this suggested that he truly had my best interests at heart. So I did – marry him, three weeks later. And we did it properly. My white lace dress was unique. Mike helped me design it and cut out the pattern in newspaper. I was still sewing frantically an hour before the wedding.

'Don't give us any presents,' we instructed. 'We've

nowhere to put them, no prospect of a home for years. So my sister-in-law gave us six very expensive wine glasses, with big fragile bowls and long slender stems.

'Thank you so much,' we said, through clenched teeth.

We'd spent the last of our meagre savings on the rent for a squalid flat in Leeds for Christmas and New Year. There was no heating, and we couldn't afford a heater, so we spent most of the time huddled under the bedclothes. Well, what else could we do?

What next? Mike was ordered off to war – er, no, to the Isle of Mann for officer training. 'Bring just one trunk', said his marching orders. A trunk? We'd never seen a trunk. We certainly couldn't afford one. Mike asked the Commandant of his cadet force for advice, and three ammunition boxes were dropped off at our door. They looked like coffins for paupers from a Victorian poorhouse, just rough planks with big gaps between them.

Mike packed his few possessions into one of them and strapped his fencing foil on top. He looked quite like Errol Flynn, so maybe imagined himself playing Scaramouche. Off he went.

I packed the precious glasses in the towels a more thoughtful guest had given us. They took up an amazing amount of space in box number 2, which my poor parents somehow manhandled on the bus to Huddersfield. My long-suffering landlady welcomed me back and let me keep box number 3 under my bed.

My next summer vacation was idyllic. Mike wangled a posting to an RAF camp near Grantham and they found us a tiny cottage beside the airfield.

'We've got real furniture and knives and forks – we're playing house,' we bragged.

'Are you using my glasses?' asked my sister-in-law.

'Of course, every night,' I lied.

'But they're meant just for special occasions,' she said.

'We're having lots of special occasions.' Another lie.

In truth they were in the ammunition box in my father's little shed in Huddersfield, while we spent our time chasing hares around the airfield, or being experimented on by men training to be chefs in officers' messes.

A year later my degree course came to an end. Mike, now stationed near Blackpool, rented a flat for us in Lytham. We had to get our few possessions together. Big logistics problem: how to get two ammunition boxes across the Pennines. Well, the government that had caused our problems offered a solution. The Suez war had cut off our petrol supplies, so, to save fuel, they had banned driving tests but decreed that learners could drive unsupervised. Incredible? Absolutely. True? Absolutely. Every idiot who could scrape a deposit together bought a set of wheels, clapped on L plates, and took to the road. It was carnage out there.

We needed something big enough for the ammunition boxes. (Don't ask!) We bought a clapped out Bedford van from a farmer who'd abused it. 'It's big enough to live in if we're ever homeless,' we said.

L plates on, a book on how to drive a car, and we were off, with my box aboard. On the fifteen mile drive from Leeds to Huddersfield we more or less got the hang of driving forwards. We never did find reverse, or how to stop without stalling the engine.

My parents' house was on a slope. We never found the handbrake. We got the van into neutral somehow and let it slip backwards until it bumped into the kerb. Then my Dad rushed out with bricks to jam under the tyres.

The van was still there next morning, so on with box number 2.

'I'm going to the sea side,' yelled my little sister. We'd all learned not to thwart her, so in she climbed, on top of the ammunition boxes. Seat belts? Unheard of in 1958. She didn't even have a seat.

There were no decent roads over the Pennines then, just narrow strips of tarmac and chippings, with a camber perversely sloping in the wrong direction. Round endless hairpin bends we trundled, not always on the right side of the road. But the god of drunks and idiots must have been enjoying the ride, for we arrived unscathed, though a few other road users must have been traumatised.

My little sister emerged, shaken, stirred and black and blue, demanding tweezers to pull out the splinters.

'The sea, the sea! Take me to the sea!'

'Okay, okay, anything for a quiet life.'

So, what happened next? We couldn't sell the van, but a garage accepted it as a deposit for a car. We weren't sorry to see it go.

The ammunition boxes? Must have gone on somebody's bonfire. They were far too big for the dustbin.

The glasses! The glasses? Well, they survived the journey – unfortunately. We always hated them: they were a nasty yellowy colour. I think they must have just – evaporated.

1111 words

Yes, it's another true story.

+ + +

TASK: Write about the cottage of your dreams.

EEL PIE ISLAND

Eel Pie Cottage, Eel Pie Island. What an address! Tons more romantic than a semi in Twickenham, you must admit.

'I can't take you to see it today,' said the house agent. 'I'll ring you when I've managed to fix a boat.'

If we'd been merely young and foolish, instead of wet behind the ears and daft as brushes, those words would have snuffed out the idea on the spot – but thereby hangs a tale.

Nobody would even discus a mortgage for the impossibly picturesque little shack that shared the romantic island in the middle of the Thames with a few similarly charming wrecks. But we were in the money. Aunt Maud's legacy was almost enough.

'This is all we have,' we explained hopefully. 'Your clients will have to take it or leave it.'

They grabbed it. The cottage was ours within a week.

We drove our tiny Austin A35 to the landing stage marked 'Eel Pie Island Ferry' in fading letters. We waited and waited.

'What time is the next ferry?' we asked the nearest native watering his garden.

'Ferry? You'll have a long wait for that. It's a good fifteen years since the last one came back from over there. That was when the hotel closed down at the start of the war.'

Our search for a ferry now morphed into a search for shelter for the night. The kindly owner of the B&B had newly grown up idiot children just like us. She grinned knowingly and phoned the local boatyards until she managed to find a cheap little boat we could afford.

The boatyard owner towed the little dinghy to the landing stage for us and we loaded our few possessions on board and pushed off. I immediately lost an oar, but the current somehow washed it against the boat and Mike grabbed it. We'd never rowed a boat before, so this one went around in circles, until Mike realised he needed to match his stroke to my much feebler efforts. The current swept us right on past the island, and we were exhausted by the time we had managed to fight our way back to our little shack.

We tied up to a big tree root and unloaded our things. Something went overboard with a heavy splash. We had no idea what it was and we never saw it again.

Our neighbours came out to help and welcome us to their tiny community. The nice old couple lived in Birmingham. The boisterous family on the other side had a semi in Twickenham. The shacks were holiday homes.

'I'll lend you a lamp,' said the old man. 'The power's down again. Probably be weeks before they get around to laying a new cable across the river bed. Put it in the kitchen. As long as you can see what you're eating you should be okay.'

Rowing up the river to the nearest grocery shop was great fun – until the rain began. We struggled home, shivering and soaked to the skin. All the paper bags soon melted and the contents made cold stew in the bottom of the boat. (There were no plastic bags in the 1960's, of course, and no mobile phones either.)

Next door's children were heartily sick of the rain. What fun to lighten up a dull day by untying our boat and then cheering as it was carried off downstream by the current! Thank goodness they had a motor boat. It took their father two hours to locate our boat and tow it back. The family went home to Twickenham next day.

When the rain had continued non-stop for two weeks the old couple left as well. We tied our boat up with an extra rope, now it was the only one left on the island.

Well, we were now king and queen of our own little kingdom. The other shacks were locked and shuttered, but we managed to get into the disused hotel. The walls were painted with glamorous scenes of night life in the 1930's, before the war had taken all the fit young men and women away to fight for their country. There were lots of photos, too, and many of the people looked familiar. Presumably they must have been famous then.

We sat on the verandah and imagined ourselves part of that scene, when the rich and elegant had all the world's glamorous pastimes and places to themselves. We felt like trespassers, with the rain dripping through the ruined roof and splashing onto our heads. Unlike those idle rich we had a living to earn. Better go home and work out how we were going to get to our new jobs in Twickenham in a week's time.

'You're not allowed to tie up here,' said the native, when we set out next morning to reconnoitre. 'The trip boats sometimes stop here. They'd crush that tiny boat.'

'Well, where can we tie up, then? It says Eel Pie Island Ferry.'

'You're not the ferry. This jetty's reserved for the passenger ferry.'

'Let's find somewhere else,' said I, seeing Mike growing angrier and angrier. 'We don't want to be labelled troublesome neighbours.'

We managed to manoeuvre the boat into an inconvenient gap on the side of the jetty away from his garden, then fled when he went indoors.

'I'm terribly sorry but I'll have to ask you to find somewhere else to park your car,' said the nice B&B lady. 'I need the space for my guests.'

Oh. Quick change of plan: find somewhere to park the car. We drove in and out of every street in the neighbourhood, but all the car parks and streets banned overnight parking, and so did the landing stage.

'Should we get rid of the car and go to work by boat? We'd need somewhere to moor in Twickenham near public transport.'

Most of the Twickenham river bank said 'No Mooring' in big stark letters. The public moorings had long waiting lists. And there were no buses going near our respective workplaces either, so we'd either have very long walks to work or huge taxi bills – if we could get a mooring.

We drove home with the wipers going full tilt and our spirits at rock bottom. We slid the car quietly up to the landing stage, crept out and shut the car door quietly, then crept into the boat.

It was hard to recognise our home. We could now row right up to the verandah and tie up to the railings.

It was cold and dark, so an early night seemed the only option. Few people had a TV set then, and anyway we still had no electricity. We heaped all our warmest clothes on top of the bedclothes and burrowed into the heap, then lay listening to the wind howling, and nameless loose things flapping.

Who on earth was banging on our door in the middle of the night? Mike staggered sleepily to the door and opened it. He was nearly knocked over by the surge of water rushing in. A tree trunk barged in and wedged the door open .

'Come on,' yelled Mike. 'We'll have to get out or we'll drown. Grab this! He passed me a warm coat off the bed and struggled into one of his own.

We pulled and pulled but the back door wouldn't open against the force of the water surging against it.

'The window!' I yelled.

Thank Goodness it was a sash window.

Mike climbed through it in a flash and reached back to drag me after him. 'Hang onto the window frame, or we'll get washed away,' he shouted. 'This water's rising fast. We've got to get up on the roof.'

How I got up there I can't imagine. Mike must have pushed and pulled me most of the way. We lay flat on the roof so the wind couldn't easily blow us off.

'Oh my God, Look!' I wailed. The shack next door tore itself away from its flimsy foundations and floated away like Noah's Arc. Would ours be next? 'The tree. Let's try to climb across into the tree. Surely it's too big and strong to be washed away.'

'Have you much experience of climbing trees?' he asked. 'Harder than it looks, unless you happen to be a squirrel, and the rescue boat wont be able to reach us with all the branches sticking out.'

'They'll have to use a helicopter. I'd love a ride in one of those.'

'Did they have helicopters in those days? Anyway, they'd have even more trouble with the branches than the boat. They'd get tangled in the tree like a wasp in your hair.'

'Bzzzzzz! Bzzzzzzz! Help! Help!'

We were both laughing so much most people in the restaurant were glowering at us disapprovingly.

'If poor old Aunt Maud really had left us a legacy, do you think we would have been idiotic enough to buy that rotting little shack on Eel Pie Island?' I asked.

'Well, a fool and his money,' said Mike, 'And we were unbelievably daft in those days, Lucky we were absolutely skint, wasn't it?'   1514 words

TASK: Write a story where a character gets what he or she deserves.

THE INTERPRETER

'Am I right to infer that you have absolutely no experience of this kind of work?'

She had his full attention now – and immediately wished that she hadn't. She was no longer just one of the group of attendants involved in the exhibition: she was now the sole focus of an icy stare.

Her nod of acquiescence produced such a scowl that she felt her thin veneer of confidence begin to crumble.

'Well, not exactly – I mean that this is my first real assignment, but I've had plenty of very good practical experience as part of my course of training: the United Nations and the EEC, and a sales conference for Consolidated Confectionery.' It sounded good enough, she reasoned, clutching at the remains of her self-respect. She took a determined breath and looked him firmly in the eye. 'Everyone has to start somewhere.'

The glacier-blue eyes lanced through her fragile defences, tightening her stomach into a sickening knot.

'So, you thought you'd cut your teeth on IIT, did you?'

'I'm sure it will be very good experience,' she began, but his gasp of disbelief almost unnerved her, 'and a tremendous challenge,' she added quickly, in a vain attempt to mollify him.

'I don't think you can be fully aware of what you've taken on,' he continued coldly. 'This is one of our most important conferences. We've had acceptances from more than seven hundred people, all of them very senior executives from Europe's most important business organisations. We lead the world in Information Technology and this conference is designed to show what we can do. One little slip, one little muddle, one little hint of incompetence could be enough to shake our reputation, and the competition is always snapping at our heels. Conveying information is our business. We cannot afford to be associated with anything second rate.'

Her wave of anger was refreshing, and Heather faced him squarely. 'I am fully aware of the importance of IIT, and will be proud to be associated with the success of your conference. Now, Mr Evans, if you will give me a transcript of your lecture and time to scan it through, I shall be happy to give you an oral translation as soon as you can spare the time to listen. It's clearly important that I reassure you about my competence as a translator. It may interest you to know that I was awarded a distinction at the end of my course of training,' she concluded firmly.

'And when was that? Last week?' he snarled.

'Yes,' she countered defiantly. 'Last week.'

For a moment the ice in his eyes seemed to melt and an exasperated grin tugged at his mouth.

'Well, let's have all the bad news,' he demanded, thrusting his hands into his pockets. 'What about your colleague? Is she straight from college too?'

'The bureau asked me to give you their abject apologies,' she began, steeling herself for the storm to come. 'They had the greatest difficulty in finding the number of translators you requested. This is such a big conference. They tried all the other agencies and brought in all their available people but there just weren't enough French translators to go around. I'm afraid I shall have to cope with your session on my own.'

She mentally closed down her ears like a cat in a thunder storm, and waited for his inevitable rage. Sure enough, a sharp intake of breath was followed by a few unrepeatable exclamations.

'No, this isn't good enough,' he finally exploded. 'I must get onto that bureau of yours.'

'Mr Evans!' she called hurriedly, as he turned to stride away. 'Your lecture notes. I can start work on them while you're dealing with the bureau. I understand your presentation begins at 11am tomorrow, so that doesn't give me a great deal of time.'

He swung around and stared at her crossly. 'That's impossible, I'm afraid.'

She stared at him, puzzled and apprehensive.

'I don't read my lectures, don't you understand? I can't bear listening to people who do that. They put me to sleep. I want my talks to sound spontaneous. That's the way to engage an audience, get them onboard with you. I have the structure in my head, of course, and a few important headings on a post card to make sure I don't leave out anything important. A copy of that postcard would make no sense at all to anyone else.'

Heather fought hard to hide her consternation. There was nothing to be done about it: she would just have to go in cold. This was her worst nightmare. The question session at the end of a lecture was always a minefield for an interpreter. Preparation was nearly impossible, so it was always a terrible strain, but this! It was going to be like one interminable question time, but worse. Every thing he uttered would be new to her. She would have to start her translation of every sentence before she knew where his words were leading.

'It may be wise to add a few extra words to your postcard,' she said, 'such as "slow down, translator working."'

He studied her silently for a few agonising moments. 'I presume you have been briefed about our industry. You can distinguish a micro chip from a hard drive.'

Heather swallowed hard. 'It might be wise to give me a list of very technical terms you will be using in your lecture. I have a very good glossary of words concerned with computers and I'll make sure I have learned any others you intend to use.'

'And all before 11.00 am tomorrow,' he sneered. 'And

what will you do after breakfast? Translate all our sales literature into Mandarin Chinese and still have time for a swim? And when do you think I'll have time to make you this mile long list? I've a thousand things to do before the conference gets underway tomorrow. This is a ridiculous situation and it just isn't going to work. I'm going to tell those incompetent idiots in your bureau where they get off. They'll have to find me someone who knows what she's doing or I'll put them out of business.'

Heather glanced quickly at her watch. Her smile of wicked satisfaction stopped him in his tracks.

'You think this is funny, do you?'

'The best of British,' grinned Heather. 'The bureau closed half an hour ago. May I suggest you just ban French speakers from your session. I don't expect they'll be surprised. It will only confirm their view that the British are a lot of chauvinistic pigs with no consideration for anyone except themselves. Goodbye, Mr Evans. I hope I wont bump into you again.'

                                                1124 words

TASK: As a contrast
Write a story in which a character earns a reward

CASH FLO

'She doesn't say much, your housemaid.' The visitor gave Flora a teasing grin.

Flora put down the tea tray and stared at him, wondering what kind of response was expected of her.

As always, Mr Pettigrew was quick to rescue her. 'He is only trying to be friendly, my dear. Don't you worry. I'm sure you wont mind my explaining to my friend that you suffer a little from autism, though you are such an excellent housekeeper I'm sure no one would guess you had any health problems at all.'

'Well, now, that's very interesting,' asserted the guest. 'Hey, she might be good at figures. They often are, you know.' Tact was obviously not his strong point. 'Let's try her out. What's her name?'

Mr Pettigrew's smile had hardened. 'I'm sure Flora would rather get on with her work in peace,' he said firmly. 'Thank you, my dear.'

'Hey, Flora, what's 71 times 396?' the visitor shouted after her.

'34,116,' replied Flora softly, as she closed the door.

'Good grief, did you hear that?' he exclaimed, so loudly that Flora could hear him right through the door.

It was a day or two before Mr Pettigrew very gently and tactfully asked her if she might find it interesting to help him with his figures. Gingerly she sat down beside him and diffidently tried to make sense of the calculations on the computer screen. Percentages and basic arithmetic. Oh, yes, she could understand things like that perfectly well. It was much more fun than the housework, especially when a calculation seemed to hit a roadblock in her mind and shout, 'Wrong! Wrong!'

'Oh dear!' said Mr Pettigrew. 'However did I make a silly mistake like that? Thank you so much, my dear. Now, can you spot any more mistakes?'

Flora was soon promoted from checker to compiler of the original sums. She could, it seemed, calculate pretty well anything instantly with absolutely no danger of errors. Mr Pettigrew now had more time to read the financial papers. He seemed to find them ever more exciting. Then he doubled her wages and began buying new things for the house. What was he doing to make all this spare money so suddenly, she wondered. The newspapers beside the computer screen seemed to be the key. She stopped throwing them away and took them up to her bedroom. He had circled lots of things with a red marker, so she knew where to look. He seemed to be buying shares in companies, then selling them after a few days or weeks when the price had risen. He couldn't know the prices were going to rise, surely. He must be just guessing. Was this gambling?

The staff at the orphanage had said gambling was a dreadful sin. Was she helping a gambler, and was that a wicked thing to do? But were the people at the orphanage qualified to judge a very law-abiding, good kind man like her employer? He was in charge of her now. She should forget the orphanage and listen to him.

Soon Flora was devouring the financial pages with avid interest. When she could not resist offering advice, however, she was rewarded with a look that put her firmly in her place. What on earth could an autistic housemaid from an orphanage possibly know about high finance? Flora had to content herself with working out the figures and entering them on the screen.

Then Mr Pettigrew bought himself a fine new computer. 'I'm sure you would enjoy having my old one for yourself, my dear,' he said. 'We can fit it up in the kitchen. It has lots of games you might enjoy, and you can ask Google for any information you could wish for.'

Flora lost interest in the games when she realised how ridiculously easy they were, but she discovered that Google could find her information about all the shares she was buying and selling for Mr Pettigrew. Then life became very exciting. She was bursting to tell him about shares she was sure would do well, or badly, but he was having none of that. Her job was to do the arithmetic. His was to exercise judgement.

The great crash of 2007 was a sore trial for both of them. Rigid with apprehension she entered the figures as he instructed, despite her deep misgivings, and watched helplessly as all the profits turned to losses. It was no surprise to her when he sat with his head in his hands in deep despair.

It was a great shock, however, when he finally came into her kitchen with tears in his eyes, to explain as kindly as he could that she would have to leave, as he could no longer afford to pay her wages.

'You don't need to pay me, sir,' she said quietly. 'I don't need any more money. I'm just glad to have a nice home and a kind employer.'

Mr Pettigrew got out his handkerchief. 'That is most kind of you, my dear. I'm very touched, but that's not the end of it. I owe so much money to the bank they are going to take over my house and sell it to repay all my debts. I have had to ask the council to find us rooms in a hotel. But don't you worry. My friends are trying to find you a nice job, and I'm sure something good will turn up.'

A man with a clipboard strode from room to room making notes about everything of value. He was quite abrupt with Mr Pettigrew but seemed sorry for Flora. She made him a cup of tea, and he came into her kitchen to drink it and stayed till he'd finished his report. She managed to look over his shoulder and see the totals he had written. She had no need to write them down; she was sure she would not forget.

Going out was quite an ordeal for Flora, but she knew her way to the bank. Mr Pettigrew had taken her there to open an account he could pay her wages into. The manager came out of his office to greet her with a smile that didn't look real. He was leaning down towards her and waving his arms like an incompetent actor on TV. What did this mean? Why were people so hard to understand?

Sure enough, once she was seated in his office, he tried to persuade her to lock all her money away for ten years. He was sure it would be worth seven times as much by then. When a thing looks too good to be true it usually is. She had read that advice so many times.

'No thank you,' she said. 'I'll just do what I came for.'

'Well, my dear, I'm afraid the house has been sold, so we shall have to start packing up our things, ready to move out,' said Mr Pettigrew, looking oddly cheerful.

No, thought Flora. He looked odd, but not cheerful, just pulling his mouth sort of sideways.

No, sir,' said Flora with a decisiveness that startled him. 'I am not going to stay in a hotel. I want to stay here. And I want you to stay here as well. I should be frightened here all on my own.'

'Oh, my dear, if only we could, but we just can't.'

'We just can, sir,' said Flora. 'Look, sir.'

She opened the file of papers on the kitchen table. The new owner of number 56 Bankside Terrace was Florence Smith.

1261 words

TASK: Write a poem about a person.

LA GIOCONDA MONA LISA

An enigmatic smile; a quiet face.
Dear lady, why do you bewitch us so?
Even your very name's a mystery.
Are we mistaken, is that why you smile?
You may not be that merchant's wife at all;

How could you guess Leonardo, painting you,
Might bring you fame; but, true to form, he'd not
Complete the work for you? You never saw
It finished. He just kept it for himself.

You, whom millions crowd around to view,
Most famous work of art in history,
Lived out your quiet life in ignorance
Of the eternal fame awaiting you.

Your sweet plump face looks innocently out
Through bomb-proof glass.
'A woman good and true
Is worth far more than rubies.' You, my dear,
Are literally priceless, uninsurable.

'But she's so very plain! The picture's small
And dark and nothing special. Why the hype?'

'Where are the rings, the jewels that I wear?
Where is the pearl-strewn netting from my hair?'

Incompetent restorers cleaned them off.
The gold and silver flowers on your frock
Have faded too. Your neatly dressed dark hair
And unassuming dress signal a maid
And not her mistress. You'd be mortified.

Or maybe you'd just smile your placid smile.
At peace with life, contented with your lot.
Are you the meek, inheriting the earth?

NOTE

Did you note the changes in style? Flo and the Mona Lisa both seem gentle, unworldly people, so a gentle unworldly style seems appropriate for them,

The conference leader and the interpreter are worldly and confident, so need a style to match.

TASK: The next poem is rather creepy. Can you write a poem with that slight air of menace masquerading as innocence?

THE MEEK SHALL INHERIT THE EARTH

I envy you your golden curls,
Your eyes that sparkle like the sea;
I envy you your legs that walk,
That take you where you want to be.

I'm lighter than a feathered seed,
Smaller than anything you see,
You wont mind if I hitch a lift -
You'll never even notice me.

Stretch out that dainty little hand,
Pick up that cupcake iced in pink,
Convey it to your pretty mouth.
Now, bite and chew and swallow me.

Pity you're turning up the heat.
I liked the temperature before.
But never fear, I'll sweat it out.
I've done that many times before.

I wish you wouldn't swallow stuff
That makes me cringe and writhe with pain.
It does no good. I slough it off
And soon I'm feeling fine again.

Have you not heard the saying that
What doesn't kill you strengthens you?
This world's now fine, my progeny
Increases exponentially.

The temperature's gone down again.
Disaster strikes. In worlds like this,
So cold and still we cannot thrive.
And aliens now are pouring in.

They seem to like the awful stench
Of rotting flesh. We don't agree
With them, so sadly now we know
We need another place to go.

* * * * *

There was a young lady from Leeds
Who swallowed a packet of seeds.
No, her head didn't sprout,
An no one said nawt
Though her legs were all covered in weeds.

A Manchester girl with a stutter
Got so drunk that she fell in the gutter.
Her friends said, 'Run quick,
She's going to be sick,
And we don't want to deal with such clutter.'

UNINTENDED CONSEQUENCES

TASK: Write a story where things do not go according to plan.

Here are two stories on that theme, so now you can pretend there are three of you in the imaginary class and compare all three stories. Write yours first.

IT'S THAT MAN AGAIN

I hoped never to see that man again. He'd made my life a misery for months. He was talking to a minion, but I felt his eyes following me as I headed for the door.

'Au revoir!' he called, with a sardonic smirk.

'Hasta luego!' I called back, trying to look innocent. Adios! I added silently. No way do I ever want to set eyes on you again.

I showed my papers and walked steadily through the door, suppressing the urge to run. I could see Joe's car beyond the gate. Don't run, just walk slowly, calmly. Don't do anything to set the pigeons aflutter. This was all too good to be true: That lawyer had worked miracles.

Joe pushed the passenger door open for me and I threaded myself into the seat. 'Don't you ever clean this effin car out? Looks like a rubbish bin,' I grumbled. 'Get one of those cans jammed under the brake pedal and you're stuffed.'

'You can clean it out tomorrow, in lieu of the fare,' he laughed. 'Haven't seen you for months and you're nagging at me already like an old fish wife.'

'Okay, okay, live in a midden if you like. So, what's on the agenda?'

'We've got some stuff to unload. Need to play the door-to door salesman, do a round of all the fences. You could do the old faces down in Brixton.'

Good, I thought, that's right, just go back to the old racket, just as everybody expects. Pick up Rozzy, or failing her, Sandra. Settle in. All back to normal.

I stuck it for a month, plodding about, finding homes for assorted bits of loot; not too much in one place, nothing that looks like a big haul. The Fuzz don't have time for the small stuff these days.

'Like a nice meal tonight, Rozzy?' I said casually. 'New restaurant opened in Sawdust Alley. Belongs to old mates of mine.'

And a great evening we made of it. Franco and Guy had done the place out a treat. What a good way to launder that foreign bank job! Most of it went into the back pockets of builders and their armies of illegal immigrants. They'd no papers, see, so beyond the reach of the law and the taxman. We joined in the Karaoke. It was a great place to celebrate a job well done, and soon we were regulars, part of the furniture.

Lunchtimes were packed, loads of stuffed shirts from the offices round about. I watched the ebb and flow of people, day in, day out. The busiest time was from twelve-thirty to two, as a fuss of financiers dressed like undertakers hurried out for lunch, then rushed back to their offices again. I waited for a wet day and put up a big umbrella. That should flummox the spy cameras.

Couldn't believe how well it went: got the contents of the deposit box without a hitch, and went back for pud.

'You've been a long time in the loo,' said Rozzy.

'Gippy tum,' I said. 'Let's have another glass of vino.'

Now, how to get out of the country. Planes are too dodgy: would have to book on the internet, and GCHQ have their claws deep into that, and into airport security.

Wearing a smart dark suit and carrying only a briefcase, I went to St. Pancras and booked a Eurostar to Paris, intending to get off at Lille and head for Amsterdam. You can get to absolutely anywhere from Schiphol.

Only another half an hour to wait. I stood as calmly as I could, staring at the destination boards.

'Fancy meeting you here, Laddy,' said a voice in my ear. 'Thanks for finding us the loot.'

I felt the handcuffs, cold and hard, closing around my wrists as he relieved me of the briefcase.

                                                      634 words

THE INTERVIEW

There were six of us, as usual. And what a motley crew! The bran tub must have been almost empty when they pulled us out. For a while we sat silently in a circle, trying not to look at each other. At last the silence was shattered. A small, red-faced man bustled in and looked around fiercely.

'Mrs Donnelly? Mrs Catherine Donnelly?'

A tall, big-boned woman staggered to her feet. Her handbag slid to the floor and she scrabbled frantically to trap the lipstick that rolled off under her chair.

'Come this way, please,' ordered the man.

When the door closed we breathed a collective sigh. One down, five to go.

'Can we guess who's next,' I suggested. I can't bear silence – just have to shatter it somehow. 'We're probably being slaughtered in alphabetical order. Anyone with a name earlier than D?'

The other four came to life. One glowered at me, one laughed and two – well they were just manufactured to be spectators. Nobody owned up to a name in advance of a D.

'So,' I continued merrily, 'Anyone with a name beginning with E? F?

Silence.

'G – yes, Gossamer, that's me. Jenny Gossamer.'

'Oh, what a pretty name! Sounds like a fairy, a friend of Tinkerbell.'

At last, everyone was giggling - one of my favourite sounds. The ice seemed well and truly broken. We exchanged names and pedigrees until the man returned, dragging a limp-looking Catherine Donnelly.

'Good luck, Tinkerbell,' I called, as she was led off to the slaughter.

People often give me disapproving looks. I stick them in my mental scrapbook to wallow in at any dull moment.

We grilled Catherine Donnelly, of course, but she seemed too shell-shocked to form a coherent narrative. Silence descended. I can't have that.

'Do you know much about this school?' I asked. Everyone shook their heads. Oh, goody good!

The school I worked in was only three miles away. This one was our twin, and we had two part-timers who worked in both schools, so we heard all the staff room gossip. 'Only last week the star villain of this place, Dusty Millar, threw another girl right down a flight of thirteen concrete steps. She knew the girl was epileptic, but she didn't care. The Deputy Head has to stand guard in the cloakrooms at the end of every day to stop Dusty and her gang pushing girls' heads down the loos.'

'No!' shrieked Catherine Donnelly.

'And that's not the half of it,' I said enthusiastically. 'The Head left because he couldn't keep order. Then the woman Deputy resigned because of all the agro. Whichever one of us is appointed in her place will have to share a room with the male Deputy, and he's waging war on the new Headmaster. It's mayhem.'

'If this place is so bad why on earth did you apply for this job?'

What a sensible question! 'You may well ask,' I laughed. 'My husband likes to brag that he has me on the right side of his balance sheet. He saw the advert and pinned it onto me, then got me pen and paper and said, 'Come on, apply. It's nearer home. Save petrol.'

To shut him up I sent for application forms. Previous experience: supply teacher, further education teacher, English teacher at the school's twin. Management experience: nil. I certainly wouldn't have called this woman to interview. What must the competition be like? Anyway, with not the remotest chance of getting the job I was enjoying the experience. And I was missing my least favourite classes, the ones I coloured red on my timetable.

'Mrs Smith!' My turn. It was fun, basking in the rapt attention of a dozen pompous-looking people.

I retreated merrily to the anteroom and studied the reactions of the others. It was a fun morning out.

After the last candidate returned things became rather boring. Everybody else seemed tense. Waiting is a form of torture, wrack not needed.

'Mrs Donnelly!' said the official portentiously.

The rest of us breathed out noisily. Huh! Off the hook. None of us would have to take on this poisoned chalice. We could consign the awful Dusty Millar and the demon Deputy to the realms of hearsay. I could go home and put on a sad face. 'Sorry, Darling. I did try.'

'Would the rest of you be kind enough to wait a few more minutes?' said the official. 'I'm sure you would all like some tea. It's on the way.'

Before the tea appeared the door opened again. Catherine Donnelly, grim-faced and on the verge of tears, stalked in, picked up her coat and stormed out.

'Mrs Smith,' said the man, 'Please step this way.'

794 words

This proved a most exciting job. When things could not be worse there is so much you can do to improve matters. It is much harder to take on a good school, prevent it from deteriorating, then make it even better.

TASK: Write a poem about a school.

THE HEATHROW SCHOOL OF SINS

We have no rules against the ancient sins.
Here, as the planes roar down above our heads,
Our sins are worldly, more immediate.
They have an instant impact, shattering
The well-oiled order of our daily grind.
'Why did the teacher turn you out of class?
I'll take you to apologise to him
And see if he will take you in again.
A football match is no excuse to truant.
Cheating's not the way to pass exams
And idleness will ruin your career.'
'Please Ma'am, he's thrown my kit up on the roof.'
'He pulls my hair.' 'She stabs me with a pen.'
'He's scribbled on my homework, scoffed my lunch.'
'She thumps me for no reason, just for spite.'
'I don't!' 'You do!' So, now, who's telling lies?

Who's covered the loo walls with shocking words?
Who put these evil racist posters up?
Who pinched the money for the theatre trip?
Removed the screws from all the classroom chairs?
'Who ordered this poor 'Strippergram' to come
For Mr Smithers' birthday? Somebody must pay
The poor girl for her trouble. Now, cough up.'

Who parked that stolen sports car by the gymn?
It roared around the playground going so fast
That no one saw the driver. Forensics say,
'How can we fingerprint three thousand hands?'

'There's knives out in the western playground,
Ma'am.'
Put down my break-time coffee, clap my hands,
Shout, 'Year Heads, please, I need you, follow me!'
Stride out ahead of my Praetorian Guard.
The seething crowd of Sikhs has spotted me.
Mohinder and Rupinder, film star looks,
Their beards twisted into ropes and tied
Beneath their turbans, innocently smile.
'A nice day, Ma'am. Is that a jumbo jet?'
'A Boeing 707, boys. That engine note
Is like an orchestra.' The Sikhs, I've heard
Wear ceremonial daggers in their socks.
I could strip-search the lot of them. Oh, wow!
Mohinder and Rupinder! What a thought!

And now I teach a lesson for a change.
Hope nobody will drag me from the class,
Insisting that some crisis cannot wait.
Some teachers *cause* disruption, turn a class
Of quiet willing kids into a mob
Rampaging uncontrolled around the room.
They send a note to me: 'please come at once.'
I open the door, kids stand and smile at me.
Whatever is the problem? They're just lambs.
'This class wont listen to me. You must make
Them settle down and do the work I've set,'
Demands the teacher, outraged and distressed.
I have no magic wand. It took me years
To earn co-operation and respect.
There's no fixed formula. You have to find

Your own approach, try many strategies -
Or maybe this profession's not for you.
The queue outside my office rarely shrinks.
Another store detective, looking grim,
Tips out a pile of loot onto my rug.
(Refrain from saying, 'Didn't she do well!
We've never seen her show such enterprise.')

Airport police? I've not met them before.
'He'd climbed into the baggage hold? Oh, dear!'
(A shame you found him. He'd be gladly missed.)
'Lucky he isn't ISIS or the IRA!'
Railway police, now. That's another first.
'Stoning the trains? Oh dear, whatever next!'

'Come in, Dear. Tell me why you look so glum.'
She's pregnant, aged thirteen. The father is
Her brother. Call Social Services again.

This foreign teacher's work permit's expired.
He's banned from work forthwith. And now
A Science teacher's threatening to resign.
Teachers are gold dust. Pray some more from Oz
Are on the next plane heading for Heathrow.

The four o'clock bell sounds, the queue's still long.
The building empties as I struggle on.
Drag myself home too tired to eat, and then
Tomorrow I will do it all again.

   P.S. All the above things really happened – but not all on the same day, thank Goodness!

TASK: Write a story about hypnosis

HOWZAT, PAUL MCKENNA?

How many people can Paul McKenna hypnotise at once? I've no idea. Seven hundred and fifty?

The Head called me in. 'I'm hearing worrying rumours.'

I knew what he was getting at: I'd heard the same rumours myself: the staffroom was buzzing with them. To mark the last day of the Summer Term, ie, tomorrow, the kids were planning a bit of devilment to wind up the teachers. At the end of the day they planned to make the biggest possible mess of their form rooms, then scarper. About four hundred of the older ones were leaving for work or college. The younger ones were just gung ho. 'They can't punish us till September. They'll have forgotten about it by then. It'll be a great joke.'

Ha! Ha! Who's going to clean it all up? The poor down-trodden underpaid cleaners?

He wasn't Head for nothing: he was a fine strategist. If there was a way to pre-engineer his way out of trouble he'd find it.

'I'm going to re-arrange the day,' he said. 'We're going to break the law. We wont start the day with the statutory Assembly, we'll finish with it. We'll start lessons straight away at 8.45. We'll tell the staff to give the kids something calm and structured to do. No end-of-term fun and games. They'll think we're killjoys, but we can't risk losing control of the whole school.

'I'll instruct the kids to empty all their desks and lockers today and take their property home. Tomorrow I'll ring the bells at 3.30pm to call them down to the Assembly Halls. Half the staff will attend Assembly. The other half will lock the classroom doors and all the corridor doors, then man the exits, so nobody can get back into the building. The staff In the Assembly Halls will man the fire exits and let the kids out into the playground when we give them the signal at 4.00. What do you think?'

'Brilliant!' said I. My heart had sunk down into my shoes. It was painfully obvious what was coming next.

'You and I need to brainstorm what to say to the kids in Assembly to keep them under control for half an hour.'

How would you like to face down 750 demob-happy teenagers, high as kites, champing at the bit to rush back to their form rooms and trash the school? No tasers allowed, no tear gas, no water cannon, not even a whip and a chair: nothing but words – if they could be persuaded to listen.

The Head, naturally, always took the better of the two Assembly Halls, the one that still had a stage for him to stand on. My hall had had its stage bricked up to form a drama studio. I suppose I should have made a fuss back then and insisted on a little dais to stand on, but I simply put the nearest chair against the new brick wall and climbed up on it, like a street corner orator. I usually gave it a shove before I climbed up onto it, in case the boys had taken the screws out. They usually did.

We got through the day without a riot, and at 3.30pm the Head rang the bells. Down trooped more than fifteen hundred excited teenagers plotting mayhem.

'What a wonderful year this has been,' I began.

'Hey?' signalled the 750 faces in my hall. This was a tough inner-city comprehensive, right under the flightpath into Heathrow. The great wonder was that the building was still pretty well intact and nobody had been injured – well, not seriously anyhow.

'You've all worked so hard your exam results are sure to be the best we've ever had. I can't wait to come back in August to hand you your results and compliment you all on the best grades for years.'

They stared at me open-eyed and open-mouthed. She's finally flipped her lid, their expressions seemed to say. I certainly had their attention. But they usually lent me their ears. I'd stood on a rickety chair in front of them twice a week all year, and worked hard to find something interesting to say. But God help a stranger!

In the hall next door the Head was ploughing the same furrow. We'd spent an hour brainstorming the best way to entice them to listen. Praise! Everybody loves to be praised. It was proving to be time well spent.

On and on I droned, making mountains out of every tiny little triumph, every win on the sports field, every exhibition of work, every TV broadcast we'd taken part in in. Yes, we were game for things like that.

We'd agreed we'd speak quite slowly, and without our usual animation. This time we didn't want them laughing and responding. We wanted them calm, calm, calm.

Slow down, relax, calm down, everything's okay, I told myself. I kept my body still so I didn't capsize that chair and crash-land in front of a jeering, catcalling rabble.

Things seemed to be going very well. They were the quietest and stillest audience I'd ever encountered. If they'd been adults I'd have assumed I'd bored them to sleep, but bored teenagers don't sleep: they raise Cain.

They were staring at me with open mouths. Some looked quite cross-eyed.

The bells rang for 4.00pm. My ordeal was over. In the same flat tone, I wished them a good holiday and pointed to the teachers beside the fire doors. The doors swung open, but the kids stood rooted to the spot. I waved to the staff. They took hold of the nearest kids and steered them gently out into the playground.

I watched the Hall empty, slowly, silently,

Surely I was dreaming! My knees buckled. I staggered down off the chair, then collapsed onto it. I felt as if I'd just survived a few rounds with Mike Tyson. Somehow, quite by accident, I'd hypnotised the lot. Yawooo!!

1052 words

TASK: Take two novels. Start your story with the first line on page 160 in one novel and finish with the last line on page 273 in the second novel.

A VERY RESOURCEFUL WOMAN

'Do certain things induce a feeling of importance or superiority, do you think? Your glamorous title, for instance, may add a little lustre to your dress collections.'

The Grand Duchess Olga smiled. It was, to be sure, only a ghost of a smile, a smile exuding condescension.

'Well, my dear man, when one can trace one's noble lineage way back into the mists of time, one might surely be forgiven for acknowledging one's slight – distance - from those whose position in life is, shall we say, a little less exalted.'

She laid her hands on the arms of her chair as a king might on his throne. At once the cameras zoomed in on the diamonds, the rubies, the sapphires on her glittering rings and bracelets.

Her interviewer gazed at her resentfully. Why on earth had he been lumbered with this interview? He knew nothing about fashion. He didn't want to know anything about fashion. Surely some female interviewer must be around in the studios somewhere. They should have brought her in to replace Helena. Well, thousands of people were watching, so he'd better not spoil his image by making a mess of things. He swallowed hard to try to rid himself of the urge to tip something noxious over the bouffed-up hair of this old gorgon.

'Your recent collection is causing quite a stir. Some unkind commentators have suggested that some of the garments might not be convenient for a career woman or flatter the figures of women of a normal size.'

'My clothes are not designed to flatter or please the average working woman. They appeal to the knowledgeable, sophisticated woman who has the confidence to wear such clothes with panache,' she reprimanded him.

'I'm intrigued,' said the interviewer, 'and I'm sure our viewers will be too, by the price-tags. Is there truly a buyer for a plain black T shirt priced at two thousand pounds?'

'A fine staple of any woman's wardrobe – already sold to a very glamorous, discerning customer,' she replied, fixing him with a fierce stare.

'My viewers may say they could buy fifty plain black T shirts for two thousand pounds,' he challenged.

'Ah, but do they have my name hand-stitched into the neckband? The distinguished 'ladies who lunch', as they are so quaintly called by the better magazines, are not afraid to spend their clothing allowances or their trust funds on the most prestigious labels, of which mine, I am pleased to say, is one,' she replied triumphantly.

The interviewer took a deep breath and put on a false ingratiating smile. 'I understand your life has been very hectic recently. You have presented your collections in New York, Milan, Paris and Dubai. Do you have any helpful tips for avoiding adverse health effects from so much exhausting flying?'

'Of course,' she smiled languidly, examining her long red claw-like nails. 'Turn left. Always turn left.'

'Turn left?' he queried.

'Never venture into cattle class. Never allow yourself to be hassled by the - - the crowd. Turn left, always choose Buck's Fizz rather than straight champagne and don't choose anything too hard to digest for dinner, or you may find it hard to stretch out comfortably for an untroubled night's sleep.'

The crowd! The Great Unwashed was what you wanted to say, I'll bet, thought the interviewer. 'Thank you, your Grace. I'm sure my viewers will be glad to follow your advice.'

Great big conceited pampered Persian cat, thought the interviewer. I'd love to throw you down a well and drop the bucket on you. Ding dong bell!

'So,' he said to his wife that evening, 'did you watch my programme this afternoon?'

'You were brilliant, of course, as always.'

'So, you saw the Grand Duchess Olga and her ugly sister dress collection? What did you make of her?'

'The horrid woman annoyed me so much I've been researching her on Google, and what do you think?'

'She's a fraud?' he exclaimed hopefully.

'Very probably. Few genuine high-ranking aristocrats escaped the Revolution and most of them were penniless when they arrived in the West. Her grandmother arrived in Paris weighed down with jewellery sewn into her underwear. There was a kerfuffle in 1927 when someone claimed to recognise her as the genuine Duchess's lady's maid. When nobody else came forward with evidence your Duchess's Grandmother threatened to sue the woman if she didn't stop spreading the story. She was so well off that the aristocrats were pleased to pander to her for the sake of a few good meals. She started her fashion designing to get to know a circle of wealthy people. Your Duchess is following in her footsteps. Did you try asking her how her family escaped the Revolution.

'Of course. How could I resist it?'

'And what did she say?'

'She said "**my Grandmother must have been a very resourceful woman.**"'

805 words

TASK: Write a story about someone wrongly accused of a crime

HAND ME THE VALIUM!

Time to go. If I didn't hurry up I'd be late. All night I'd tossed and turned, planning my day in Court. I'd proclaim my innocence in a firm, strong voice. They wouldn't be able to intimidate me.

If only Gwen hadn't rung to wish me luck. She meant well, of course she did, but the effect was catastrophic. I was shaking all over by the time I hung up on her. This wouldn't do at all. Valium, that's what I needed, only 2 milligrams, a sub-therapeutic dose. It had kept me safe on the ski slopes, unperturbed by the sight of a black piste falling away beneath my feet like a house-end. It would make these legal eagles look like pigeons. I rooted one out of my precious store and swallowed it. Put another in my purse? No, it was supposed to last for twenty-four hours and I know that two could make me incoherent.

Why do they keep you hanging around in the ante-room so long? Pure sadism. Wear you down, exhaust your Dutch courage.

Oh, we're on. Handbag, umbrella, notes - - oh blast! My notes have fallen on the floor. One has coasted under that bench. Get a grip, woman! No time to get them back into any kind of order. Stop thinking about them. Calm down. You've had the Valium. You'll be calm and steady as a rock.

The trial? Just a blur. The Prosecutor was a slimy thug, showing off, pretending he was acting the great hero in a Shakespeare play. For Goodness sake, it's only a pathetic little vase. Even if I had been guilty I hadn't robbed a bank, murdered a baby, hurt some-one's grandma. Harrod's should be prosecuted, not me. How dare they charge £60 for a simple little vase that cost £1 in Woolworth's? It was daylight robbery,

Now it was my Defence's turn. Steady on, you make me blush. I wish I were half as saintly as you're making me out to be. I know you're paid to exaggerate my good points – surprised you could think of any, but, you know, my good character has no bearing on the case at all. You should be telling them I'm an idiot. Who but an idiot would be naïve enough to take a vase out of a showcase in Harrods whilst clutching an identical one from Woollies in the other hand? I deserve a jail sentence for idiocy, don't I? Well, maybe I'll get one. No use fining me. I'd have to ask the bank for a loan to pay the fine and they'd turn me down with my overdraft so big already.

This woman, who is she? She's saying she recognises me. Well, I don't recognise her at all. She has a photographic memory, she says, and can remember me buying the vase six months ago. I told her I'd been given a spray of orchids for my birthday and had to put them in a jam jar. She asked the court to let her hold the vase and pointed to the tiny 'W' printed on the bottom. Harrods couldn't recognise their own merchandise, she said. Their vases were marked with a tiny 'H' by the supplier. The vase I had in my bag when I walked out of Harrods had a 'W', not an 'H'

Thank you, a thousand times, thank you for remembering me. I can't remember you from Adam.

By the time I was released she had disappeared. I'd have to make a special trip to Woollies to thank her.

'And', said my lawyer, 'I shall be writing to Harrods in the strongest terms demanding damages for you.'

'Damages? The vase wasn't damaged, was it? Not to my knowledge, anyway.'

'The damage to your reputation, the waste of your time, the risk of losing your job, your marriage prospects, your sleepless nights. We'll make them pay. You wont be out of pocket, we'll make sure of that. Can you think of anything else you want us to bring to their attention?'

My head felt like a cushion overstuffed with feathers.

'Could you steer me in the direction of a good strong cup of tea,' I answered wearily. 'I'll save the cheering and the crying till the Valium wears off.'

720 words

TASK: Write a poem about someone harbouring sinful thoughts

THE MONK

Inexorably the icy chill leaks in Through
Walls and floors and penetrates their bones,
Yet still they kneel in penance on the stones
Through days and nights, whenever the bell tolls.
The minds within the tonsured heads are full
Of sinful thoughts, their frozen bodies wracked
With noxious feelings of forbidden lusts -
 It must be so, for so the Abbot says.
This gnawing ache feels more like rheumatism,
Thinks ancient Brother Angus. Oh, Dear Lord,
Forgive me for my disobedient thoughts.
The Abbot dined so very well last night
At the King's table. Lucky, lucky man!
A dish of suckling pig. Oh, what a joy
To fill my empty belly this cold night!
Forgive my greed, Dear Lord, oh please forgive.
I must not envy him. That would be sin.
If he should make his saintly way to Heaven
Then surely I should be the chosen one
To take his place. I am more dignified
And learned far than he, and all agree.
I should have been made abbot long ago
If I had bribed the bishop, as he did.
Dear Lord, please take him up to Paradise,
Then in your wisdom give his post to me,
I'm free from sin as any monk could be.

TASK; Write a story showing someone doing something for love, whilst expecting no reward.

SHEBA

'Bang! Bang!

'What the Hell! Clear off! This is private property. Clear off or I'll shoot the pair of you.'

Luckily for them Bill was not carrying a gun, but they believed him. They scrambled out over the gate, then he heard them trying to start their engine. He leaned over the gate to memorise the number plate as their battered old wreck careered off into the distance. He'd certainly put the wind up those adolescent poachers. Strange that Sheba didn't chase them. He'd heard her howling – that's what had brought him to the copse.

'Sheba! Here, girl! Sheba, heel! Sheba? Where are you, girl?'

The only sound was a whimper.

'Where are you, Sheba? Come, Come!'

The whimpers turned to yelps and howls. He felt suddenly sick. 'Sheba, are you alright, girl?'

There she was: he could just see the tip of her nose above the bushes. Alright? She was anything but. She was struggling to get up, but her bottom seemed pinned to the ground. He knelt down among the brambles and cautiously stretched his hand to her rump. Her scream was almost human. Her thick grey fur was matted with blood. He saw the fear in her bluebell-coloured eyes.

'It's alright, Sweetheart,' he murmured, trying to comfort himself as much as her. 'We'll get you right again in no time.'

Thank God for mobile phones! 'May, listen, quick! Those bloody poachers have shot Sheba. She's bleeding badly. Get over here as fast as poss. Leave

Joe to tell the vet we're on the way, We're in the copse near the oak tree gate. Drop everything, May, for God's sake. She's going to bleed to death.'

He heard the Land rover starting up in minutes. Good old May. Two things in life he could bank on: one was Sheba and the other was May.

Once they had Sheba aboard May drove as carefully as she could, but he winced at every jolt as he nursed poor Sheba's beautiful head on his lap. Under her bushy white eyebrows her trusting eyes were fixed on his face as if she knew her life depended on him.

The vet was her usual wonderful self. The assistant hurried out with a stretcher and Sheba was in the operating theatre in minutes. The vet didn't try to turn Bill out until the anaesthetic had put Sheba to sleep. She could recognise a stubborn man when she met one.

'This is going to take some time, I guess,' said May. 'I'd better get back to the farm – left in such a hurry Goodness knows what's going on behind my back. You coming?'

'Coming home? Not without Sheba. No way!'

May knew this stubborn man all too well, so she gave him a little hug and left him to it.

It was more than an hour before the vet came out with a very long face. 'I'm afraid those blasts from the shotguns have done an awful lot of damage. It's not only her back legs, it's the spine as well. If she were human we'd be ordering a wheel chair, but, well, we don't have wheelchairs for dogs, do we? She's had a good life. She's ten. You'd be thinking of retiring her soon, in any case, wouldn't you? Best I give her another big dose of anaesthetic and let her go.'

'Let her go? My Sheba? Don't tell me I've a house full of dogs all ready to take her place. You know she's irreplaceable. She's far better than any dog I've ever trained. She's so damned clever. She works things out, she thinks for herself. You've seen her work. She could have won any sheep dog trial I dared to enter her for, but some jealous idiot would guess the truth and denounce her, then the authorities might step in. You've been very good to me and Sheba, keeping it all to yourself.'

'Why wouldn't I?' asked the vet, with a wry smile. 'It's a thrill to get so close and personal with a real full-blooded wolf. She's been a joy to deal with. I'll miss her dreadfully.'

'You're telling me she's dying? Can't you do something, anything to save her. I don't care what it costs.'

'I'm thinking of Sheba. She's a cripple now. There's nothing anyone could do to make her walk again.'

'Can't we give her a chance, hope for a miracle?'

'I'll keep her in the infirmary for a few days, see how things go, give you time to come to terms with things.'

May and Joe were just as understanding. They got on with the work while he spent far too much time in the animal infirmary. For a week poor Sheba was cross-eyed with sedatives and painkillers, but she tried to lick his hands when he came in. The second week she was wide awake and shaking her upper body, trying in vain to make her beautiful thick tail wag to greet him. The grey fur was beginning to grow again on her lower half to hide the wounds. At the end of the week the vet agreed she might as well go home.

Bill's joy didn't last for long. Whenever he put on his boots and headed for the door Sheba tried her best to follow. She yelped and whined as she struggled to drag her useless rear along the floor. He wept inwardly as he watched her helplessly.

May came up trumps again. She was looking very pleased with herself when he got home for tea. She'd found a pairs of wheels on an axle, the remains of an old pram. Joe had dug out some useful wood.

'You used to be a good carpenter. Make Sheba a

wheel chair. I'll cut this old leather coat up to make some sort of hammock for her body.'

It was trickier than it sounded. Sheba's useless legs needed a second sling to get them off the floor, but at last they had something that worked. They hugged each other as they watched her dragging her wheels behind her out into the farmyard, barking like a dog with laryngitis for sheer joy. She tried to play with the dogs, but soon toppled over and couldn't right herself. She needed a carer whenever she left the house, to stop the dogs from jumping on her playfully .

The biggest problem was the smell. The damage to her spine left her no control over her bowels. Finally the smell in the house was just too much. May insisted on moving her into the nearest barn. Every day they had to take her outside and hose her down, and clean her corner of the barn. Then she shivered in her sodden fur.

'Come listen to this,' said May eventually. She led him out to the barn. He could hear Sheba whimpering.

'We're not being kind to her. We're torturing her. If she could speak imagine what she'd say.'

'You're doing the right thing. I've no doubt about that,' said the vet. 'Go back to the kitchen. I'll join you in about five minutes.'

'No. I want to be with her. Please don't hurt her.'

'She wont feel a thing, but she'll know that you're upset and that will frighten her.'

'I'll tell her that tomorrow she'll be her old self again. We're going to set out together to round up some sheep. Will she believe me, do you think?'

'Of course she will. Just hold her head and beam that picture into her eyes.'

Sheba relaxed her aching body, yawned, then, with a deep sigh, she closed her bluebell eyes.   1290 words

TASK: Write a story showing someone doing something for love, knowing there will be no reward.

GOODBYE

She'd been a sweetheart ever since she was born. Her chubby face broke into a smile the first time he was allowed to approach her cot. The first steps she took were in his direction, while Eve was on the phone haranguing the local butcher. She'd soon rushed in to push him aside and grab the little sweetie. Then he could only watch while Eve propelled her up and down the sitting room.

'No, Darling, move the left foot now, not the right foot. No, this foot. Come along, you can do it. Isabel next door is walking far better than you.'

'Well, Isabel is three months older, Dear,' Jonathan pointed out gently. 'I think Susanna's doing very well.'

'What do you know about babies,' Eve had scoffed.

Quite a lot, actually. I am a paediatrician, after all, he thought. No point in reminding her. 'All book knowledge,' she would say. 'You men doctors talk a lot of nonsense. Mother knows best. Everybody knows that. No man can imagine what it's like to give birth to a baby, but the mother's instinct takes over straight away.'

Mmm, breathed Jonathan, thinking of the long lines of bewildered, tearful mums who begged for his advice day in, day out, but arguing with Eve was not worth the hassle, - not if he wanted peace on earth in future.

His happiest memories were the evenings when Eve was out at her committee meetings, Rotary and W.I. Then he could help Susanna with her homework. That always led to interesting discussions and kept him well abreast of current education. She truly seemed to value his opinions, and even shared her worries when relationships were not going as well as she would like.

He was thrilled when Susanna chose a university less than an hour away, so every other week she paid a visit to her old home. Some of the boyfriends she brought with her gave him sleepless nights. Eve lectured her on their shortcomings in her usual strident manner. At last his restraint was stretched too far.

'If you carry on like this she'll marry one of these louts, just to show she's not your slave.'

'Somebody has to knock some sense into her,'

'You had eighteen years to do that. She's an adult now. She has a right to choose her own friends. If we brought her up properly we should be able to trust her. If you carry on haranguing her she'll stop coming home.'

Eve pursed her lips and scowled at each new boyfriend, but she kept her bad opinions to herself.

'This is Ralph.' said Susannah, towards the end of her final year. 'He's going to be a surgeon, a paediatric surgeon, You must know doctors in that speciality. How do they cope when their patients don't pull through? Surely they must get quite upset.'

Once again he could revel in their conversations. She was right on his wavelength again. She'd chosen to study pharmacy, which seemed a little dry to him, but a son-in-law like Ralph would be a gift.

'Ralph seems a good man,' he told her. 'He treats you with respect, always tries to meet you halfway when you disagree. He's not a doormat, either – stands up for what he believes is right.' Unlike me, he thought wryly.

'Have I chosen the right man, Dad?' she asked eventually.

'Till death us do part is a very long time. Think carefully. Don't take my advice, I'm biased. He'd be a perfect son-in-law.' he smiled.

'Come see my wedding dress,' she whispered. 'Mum hates it. She's earmarked something horribly fussy.'

What a privilege, he thought as he met her in the wedding shop during his lunch break. A daughter who values your opinion on such a monumental choice. It was lovely, of course, elegant and simple, no ostentation or fussy frills.

'It's beautiful,' he said.

Eve complained loud and long when they announced the date of their wedding. It was far too soon, and, in any case, she would be away on a two week W.I. trip just when all the planning needed to be done.

Jonathan took a few days leave to help with their plans so they could concentrate on revising for their final exams. Yes, he agreed, it was a good idea to have the ceremony here in Guildford and then a blessing in Adelaide so all Ralph's family could attend. He tried not to think about Adelaide as he worked hard to perfect the arrangements for the service and the reception.

The father of the bride. He had great trouble with his speech. Eventually he bought a book of model speeches and chose the most innocuous of those. It was not that he was spooked by making speeches – in fact he was famed for his gentle wit, but this was different. What do you say when the only wonderful thing in your whole sad existence is about to walk out on you forever.

Of course there are planes to Australia. Of course he could fly out there now and then, but what could he do if she needed him? Complications in childbirth? How could he shrink all those thousands of miles in time to be of any use whatever.

If only they would stay in England! If only Eve would bite her tongue. The more she railed about a grandma's rights the keener they were to escape. Ralph said he couldn't get another visa. Maybe that was true, but he didn't seem too sad about it. He was clearly longing to go home. Susanna could talk of nothing else but the thrilling new country that was soon to be her home.

It was a relief when the wedding was over. Eve found fault with all their arrangements and stomped around glowering from dawn till dusk. Even at the airport she was listing her demands to be kept informed and consulted about all their doings.

Jonathan hugged them both. 'Be happy,' he said quietly, then watched them disappear into Departures. Then he turned and looked at Eve, with her eternal scowl.

That was the end of my life, he thought. The rest will be mere existence.

1035 words

TASK: Write a story about something that was more trouble than it was worth.

THIRTY FEET OF TROUBLE

It was a scorcher, the summer of 1976. Every day for weeks the temperature climbed above ninety degrees.

"We should have done this in the winter, as soon as we moved in," we scolded ourselves, guiltily watching the men with their miniature digger sweating profusely in our back garden, and the fleet of lorries carrying away the spoil. But when we moved in the previous autumn the idea of installing a swimming pool didn't even cross our minds. If anyone had suggested it we would have scoffed: "this is England, not the south of France. Jump into a freezing cold pool? No fear!" Born on the bleak moors of Yorkshire, we were astonished by the Greater London climate. "The South," said my father, "is another country."

Our next door neighbour, an estate agent, warned us it could make our house more difficult to sell. Pools needed constant attention and could drown people.

"We've no plans to sell, and we can swim," we countered airily. Our new house was like a giant fish tank, with floor-to-ceiling wall-to-wall windows facing due south over a golf course. The temperature in the main rooms must have been a hundred with the windows shut. A swimming pool seemed much more fun than installing air-conditioning. We had to find some way to cool ourselves.

We did our homework, and discovered that all swimming pools are not the same. If we installed the usual tile-covered concrete basin, it would be difficult to remove if we regretted it. Imagine the ear-shattering noise of pneumatic drills in our quiet close working for days to break up all that rock-hard concrete! And concrete pools, we learned, can crack and develop expensive leaks and even disrupt the natural drainage in the whole neighbourhood.. There was, however, a less permanent alternative, a hole lined with sand and a pool-shaped vinyl sheet. Sounds disgusting, doesn't it, but the samples we saw installed in show gardens were impressive, indistinguishable from concrete pools until you touched the vinyl, pleasantly smooth and warm, unlike the lumpy cold and hard ceramic tiles. To get rid of a vinyl pool you need only pull out the vinyl liner and fill up the hole with about sixteen lorry-loads of soil and rubble – that's all.

They don't tell you about potential problems, not until you already have a hole thirty feet long and six feet deep in your garden.

"We've got a tiny problem," said the foreman, when we asked about the big bulge in one side of the pool. "We need the weight of the water inside the pool to counteract the pressure of the soil outside the pool. With this hosepipe ban we don't know if we dare fill up the pool. The Water Board might fine you and cut off your water supply. Maybe our boss should talk to the Water Board."

We spent a sleepless night.

The boss soon convinced the Water Board that his business would go bankrupt if he couldn't fill up the new pools that he built, so a special dispensation was granted to us to run two hoses day and night. At last the prop stopping the sides from caving in could be taken away. The bulge had miraculously disappeared. Our new pool was the lovely oval shape we had chosen. Oh joy! Meanwhile a big alcove behind the garage had been glassed in and into this pool house cum changing room went a gas boiler, twice the power of the one that heated our whole house. It took an hour to heat the pool water one degree. We hurriedly acquired a floating quilted cover to keep the heat in. It seemed a shame to cover up the pretty turquoise mosaic pattern, but our gas bill had gone through the roof.

Our estate agent neighbour arrived with a bottle of champagne and his wife and two sons in tow to help inaugurate our pool. They were the first of a long line of uninvited guests. One morning the sound of splashing woke us. A boxer dog was swimming frantically and clawing at the vinyl walls. Mike hurtled down the stairs, jumped in and heaved the heavy struggling beast up out of the water. It shook itself and ran off - and we never discovered where it came from. Innumerable hedgehogs were not so lucky. They drowned themselves quietly and ended up nose down in the skimmers. One morning we found a mouse shivering on the top step, water up to the tops of its tiny legs. We fished it out, put it under a bush and made it some bread and milk.

When we finished landscaping the garden around the pool it was an elegant place to relax with a gin and tonic, only spoiled by the endless stream of insects determined to commit suicide by diving into the water. I did my best to fish them out, but I couldn't stay on rescue duty day and night, now could I?

One weekend we had visitors staying with us, so we left the pool boiler on all night. Next morning the men went out for an early dip and hooted with laughter, We women looked out of the bedroom windows and could hardly see through the steam – it was like a Chinese laundry. The water temperature was over 90 degrees.

The pool gave us a new angle on the world: from down in the water, eyes level with the soil, we could watch the birds pecking at the lawn from below. We had the only green lawn for miles around that first summer. No, we didn't dare to water it. We felt guilty enough about filling the pool. Our predecessors had been neglectful gardeners and left the lawn to its own devices. What little grass there had been had died in the drought, leaving only what you might call weeds and we called wild flowers. The daisies, dandelions, scarlet pimpernel, yellow trefoil, chickweed, yarrow and clover seemed to be drought-resistant. We had fun identifying them in our wild flower books and making plans to landscape the garden.

We had sited the pool along the left hand boundary wall to add interest to a featureless space. Facing it, a long line of tall fir trees marked our right hand boundary. The area in front of our windows we left fairly clear to focus on the view right up the golf course to the horizon.

Immediately outside our windows was a broad paved terrace and edging that a long narrow bed planted with scraggy mildewed roses. That ugly bed would have to go as soon as the weather broke. Eventually it broke and it went – of its own accord. Water poured down from the thunder clouds like Niagara Falls, picked up the soil from the rose bed and swept it sideways straight into the pool. When the rain stopped we had a thirty foot long bowl of rosebed soup. After a few days it turned green, greener than the lawn.

Hmm. Now what? Shock it! What it? We followed the instructions on the bottle. The pool turned brown again – for a few days. It was nearly Christmas before we could see the bottom again, after hours and hours of vacuuming, not helped by the barrow-loads of autumn leaves that collected on the cover and had to be removed very carefully so they didn't add to the soup in the pool below. Hurriedly we had the scruffy rose bed replaced by a long brick flower box half a metre tall. We made sure the soil ended a good long way below the top of that box. Even Niagara Falls was not going to wash that soil out of that box.

So, our estate agent neighbour was right: an outdoor pool is a headache, but despite all the problems we enjoyed it. Once the flowering bushes we planted around it began to flourish it was a lovely sight, and in the snow it looked delightful. We held garden parties for our staff and watched the younger ones splashing about in the pool, glamorously lit from below by the golden underwater lights. We could imagine we were in Hollywood or on the Riviera. Those were the days!

The vinyl pool was guaranteed for ten years, but showed no sign of wear when we sold the house after seventeen years. The wealthy Chinese family who bought it intended to knock our house down and build a mansion on the site. They intended to use the rubble from our house to fill up that thirty foot long hole in the garden, so their agent said.

What a good idea!   1447 words

TASK: Write another animal story.

PUZZ

'Yaooo! Yaoooo! A cat in distress. A very big cat, judging by the volume of the distress signal. Where was it? There wasn't a cat in sight. There was a row of bushes between the promenade and a garden fence. I looked over the fence: just a plain neat lawn: nowhere for a cat to hide.

'Yaoo! Yaoooo! The sound was coming from some-where near my feet. There was a plastic shopping bag under the nearest bush, an abnormal sight in squeaky-clean Marbella, where they wash the streets every few days and litter disappears in minutes. I gave it a poke, but it was empty.

'Yaoo! Yaooo!' Where are you, for Goodness sake?

It was the eyes I spotted first, big yellow eyes, surrounded by a tiny ball of earth-coloured fluff – a perfect camouflage.

Stray cats learn to be wary, but in Spain they don't usually run away. The Spanish put food out for the strays, in large quantities, so the cats only back away if you try to touch them. The kitten didn't even back away; it gazed into my eyes as I bent to pick it up, then fastened its tiny claws into my jumper.

'Could my little girl have a look at your kitten?'

'It's not my kitten. I've just found it under this bush. I need to find its owners. They'll be worried about it.'

'I don't think you'll find any owners,' said the man. 'It's probably a feral cat, born without a home. The mothers dump them on people's doorsteps as soon as they can eat solid food – hope someone will take pity on them and give them a home. You'd better take it to a vet and get it de-flead and vaccinated.'

The man was right: I knocked on doors and put notices on lamp-posts, to no avail.

Marbella is over-supplied with every possible service. including medics of all professions. There were a few Chinese shops nearby selling every small thing under the sun except food, so it was easy to find a small cat-carrier, and there was a vet in the next street. Service is usually instant as well, so the poor kitten was soon hanging by the scruff of its tiny neck from the big strong hands of the vet. Fleas cascaded down onto his metal examination table as he sprayed it long and hard with a huge can of insecticide. Next it was inoculation time for the poor little mite, then finally came a microchip with our name and address, in case the kitten got lost. It was now officially ours.

Slumping in front of the TV was no longer an option. Puzz became our chief source of home entertainment. She was hyperactive, and determined we should join in all her games. She had us leaping around the flat like demented apes. Anything and everything she could turn into a game, a toy. If we tried to stand still she would stage an attack. She crouched on her belly as far away as possible, glowered at us with her scary bulging hunting eyes, then launched herself into a charge, leapt into the air and landed smack in the middle of our chests with such a wallop that we nearly fell over backwards. How could such a tiny scrap pack such a punch?

When she realised she had tired us out, she would put on a circus act, scuttling up the curtains like a squirrel, running along the curtain poles, and leaping impossible gaps on and off the furniture - but she never knocked anything off. A favourite trick was sitting on the top of a half-open door and clawing any heads within reach.

She played solo football with those chocolates shaped like canon balls, the ones with shiny red wrappings shaped like wings, or the Snitch in Harry Potter. Kitten and chocolate went skidding merrily along our white marble floor and sometimes crashed into the walls. She could jump like a flea. We scoured the Chinese shops for toys to amuse her, and found lots of shimmering confections shaped like giant flies. She could leap into the air and bring them down from impossible heights.

We assumed she must pine for the great outdoors where she was presumably born. Obediently she draped herself around one of our necks like a collar and seemed interested in the people on the prom. Maybe she'd like to play on the sand. We sat down just out of reach of the waves and put her on the sand. She looked around, then scrambled up onto my neck, purring. Purring, we'd learned, could be a plea for help in distress rather than a sign of contentment. When we had her spayed she nestled against my neck, purring, for three nights. She must have suffered quite a lot of pain, poor thing.

She's not getting any outdoor exercise, we thought. We found a featherweight cat harness and lead. She did what every cat does instinctively when put on a lead: she rolled onto her back with her legs in the air. We tried tugging her gently along the marble floor. She rolled over and leapt up onto our shoulders. Maybe you've met a cat prepared to walk on a lead but I haven't. Why walk when you can ride on a human?

One day we met a very big dog on the prom. There seems to be a dog on every balcony in Marbella, and they never seem to cause any problems. Puzz was not to know that. She panicked, and fought her way down inside my clothes with claws fully deployed. I had to call the helicopter medics for tetanus injections. Okay, okay, this cat is now an indoor cat.

Maybe now she'd made her point she decided to have a quiet look at the great outdoors on her own. One morning she had disappeared. The only way out was a window open only two inches, three floors up above the pool deck. The caretaker insisted that no broken bodies had been spotted. For the next three days I made frequent visits to the pool deck, calling her name, then, at last she answered, and came creeping out from under a pile of deck chairs.

'I'm not going to keep you prisoner,' I told her solemnly. 'If you want to revert to the wild you're free to do so. If you want to come home, follow me.' I walked into the building and waited. Very tentatively she walked towards me, and, after a moment's hesitation while she stared into this unknown building, she suddenly ran inside and rubbed herself against my ankle. She followed me up three flights of stairs, then, when our front door came in sight, she hurtled ahead so fast she skidded on the marble and hit the door with a thump.

From then on this cat was an indoor cat. If we tried to take her out through the front door she turned into a fighting fury. The only fresh air she got was on the balcony. We felt confident she wouldn't fall off again.

'I'm terribly sorry,' said the vet, 'I seem to have misled you about the inoculations. It will be another two months before you can take the cat home to England.'

Disaster! We were going home for the summer in three weeks' time. If we put the poor cat in a kennel for six months she would probably have forgotten us or be seething with resentment when we came back in the Autumn. And we still had no plans about her living quarters in England, where the Management of our block of flats had banned all animals. We had to face facts: Puzz needed a new home.

And what a home she got! A ground floor flat with a garden, leading onto a huge communal garden that was traffic free. Her new carers sent us photos of her. She had taken over their lives, they said.

I still miss her.

1333 words

POETRY TASK: Write a poem about home thoughts from abroad

I MISS THE SULLEN SKIES

What do I miss? I miss the sullen skies:
Day after day of dismal grey,
Sapping the colour from the mournful view
Already leafless, bare, forlorn.

I miss the sullen skies
That banish defining shadows,
Slimming the dimensions down to two,
Turning the town into a cardboard set
Full of deflated people, trudging
Doggedly about their chores,
Dodging between the buildings,
Glad to get back indoors.

I miss the cold grey light that leaks
Reluctantly inside,
Too feeble to illuminate our rooms,
Or lift our gloomy, huddled indoor mood.

Here, as I watch the sunlight
Flickering on blue waves,
Oh, with the deepest of contented sighs
I miss the sullen skies.

I MISS THE WIND

What do I miss? I miss the wind.
Here, in my sunlit exile, how I miss the wind.
The wind that ploughs grey furrows in the sea,
Stampedes them headlong till they crash
Like thunder on the shore,
Then turn to fight their fellows
In a chaos of flying foam.

I miss the wind that whisks surf-riders
Scudding across the waves, like black ants
Stealing rides on one-winged dragonflies.
I miss the wind, blasting my face
With stinging grains,
Turning the promenade
Into a desert of swirling sands.

I miss the wind, rattling the rain
Against the window pane,
Moaning and sighing through
The endless winter night.

Here, in this gentle winter paradise,
Oh, what a joy it is
To miss the wind.

I MISS THE RAIN

What do I miss? I miss the rain,
That night-long rattle on the window pane.
Damp mournful drizzle that goes on and on
Till life seems grey and sodden,
Any charm quite gone.

I miss the short, sharp showers that catch you
Half a mile from home, then slyly disappear,
To leave you trudging on with clammy trouser-legs
And squelching socks, hair glued to your head,
Any pretext of sophistication laughably dead.

I miss the rain that hurtles from the thunder storm,
Fired like bullets from the great black hammer-heads,
Lit by stark lightning, leaping back into the air,
Turning the roads to rivers,
Dull drains to swirling maelstroms.

And over here, breathing this fresh dry sunlit air,
Oh, how I miss that rain-lashed indoor life.
With what smug glee
I miss the rain.

WORKSHOP TASKS

+ I Love My New Baby.

+ The Meaning of Life

+ I Miss - -

+ The Train Stopped Suddenly

+ A Misconception: Picasso's Blue Period

+ Three vases

TASK: FIRST LINE: I love my new baby

PRETTY BABY

I love my new baby. I love her to bits. She's so tiny, so helpless. Her little eyes are wide as saucers. She gazes up at me and digs her tiny nails into my arms. Sweety Pie! I've only had her three days, but she's taken over my whole life. What's on the tele? What do I care? She's far more fun to watch than anything on the screen – a laugh a minute.

Oh, someone at the door. Down you go, Poppet, sit there for a moment. Oh, hello, you've got my printer? It's working now? Well, thank Heavens for that! You can't imagine how inconvenient it's been without it.

Just put it over here. Yes, that's fine. No, don't go. I'd like to see it working first. Just wait a mo while I plug everything in. I need a copy of this thing right away. Right, here goes, cross your fingers. Oh, what's wrong? Just needs a few buttons pressed to get rid of the earlier stuff, does it? That one, cancel printing? I see.

Oh, Lord, my baby! Look, can you just get this machine going properly - - Come here, you little scamp. Gotcha! Now you just sit down here – stay! Stay! She doesn't understand plain English. Where did I find her? Here, just outside, under a bush, screaming her poor little head off. Couldn't leave her all alone, now could I? She's such a little sweety.

What did you say? She can't understand English cos she's Spanish. Mmm, hadn't thought of that. She must be Spanish, mustn't she, unless she got smuggled here in somebody's luggage. Hey, you crazy creature, come off those curtains! Yes, thanks. Careful, don't fall off that chair. Let me get a ladder. Oh, she's off again. How does she balance on top of the door? Careful, she'll try to claw your hair. I know, I'll open a tin of cat food. That might bring her down.   327 words

TASK: The meaning of life.

42

'Oh, we know all about that now, as Ford Prefect might have said in "The Hitch-hiker's Guide to the Galaxy." The mice have got it taped: it's 42.'

'What do you mean, it's 42?'

'Just plain 42. The mice built this world as a giant computer to work out the meaning of life. The world computer says it's 42, so there you have it, 42 - whatever that means.'

'So, what does it mean?'

'Oh, you know, it's just 42. Okay, so what does your brain the size of the universe tell us? No, it's 43?'

'Religions say it's just a preparation for the next world, a gateway to Paradise.'

'What kind of Paradise? One man's meat - Is seventy virgins your idea of Paradise, or singing praises all day?'

'If I'm to be one of the seventy sex slaves count me out. Let's ask the scientists.'

'If you can find two scientists singing the same tune I'll be gob-smacked. They use more energy rubbishing each other than in cutting edge research.'

'Well, I thought they had energy and all that taped, you know, E=MC squared and all that.'

'What does that mean then? E=MC squared.'

'Energy equals mass times the speed of light squared.'

'Yes, so?'

'If you can get a bit of mass to whizz about at the speed of light squared it will turn into pure energy.'

'And where do you get the energy to get anything moving at millions of miles an hour?'

'You have to blow it up, of course, in an atom bomb.

'Once you get it going how are you going to stop it? Wont it carry on and blow up all the other mass in the world and the universe and the galaxy?'

'Perhaps it will.'

'Maybe that's what they mean by the Big Bang. Some other universe blew itself to bits and all its matter came whizzing through a black hole.

'What's a Black Hole?'

'A singularity.'

What's a singularity?'

'Nobody knows.'

'Oh.'   337 words

* * * * *

TASK: I MISS - -

I miss the sea. I never dreamed I'd miss it quite so much. For twenty years it dominated my homes, probably shaped my dreams. It never paused for breath: like an animal its breathing was a constant presence, sometimes sleeping like a happy child, swish, lap, crinkle, swish, lap, crinkle. Sometime it was scary, terrifying, even, roaring like an express train thundering through an unimportant station, frightening the waiting passengers back against the walls. Usually it hit the happy medium, whoosh, thump, splash, on and on without a pause.

I wasted hours just staring at the sea, admiring its beauty, its ever-changing colours and patterns, the way the boats scored trails across it as they passed, trails that lasted long after the boats had disappeared from sight. All day the sea soaks up the sunlight, reflecting it in tiny boat-shaped glitters, then, when evening draws near, bathed by the setting sun it seems to radiate a milky turquoise light.

Often at night I watched it too. Why does the moonlight always throw a path right to your feet? Yes, I know there must be a scientific explanation, but magic seems more fun. And what of the fighting men, their helmets gleaming, marching towards the shore, to melt away to foam on the sands? How many terrified people have watched the heads rise up and stride ashore, waving swords and spears. Are these their ancient ghosts?

235 words

+ + + +

TASK: FIRST LINE: The train stopped suddenly.

Cesare stiffened, then sat back in his seat and sighed. There was no need to look out of the window. The mirrors above the seat backs reflected the views in both directions, over and over again.

They were there, of course, on both sides of the train, working their way methodically from one compartment to the next, one man climbing inside, then emerging, often empty-handed, but sometimes with an object, or more unusually with a passenger in tow, either protesting loudly or cringing silently.

He shifted his gaze to the views from the windows. The forest looked the obvious choice at first, but somebody was keeping the undergrowth in check. The tree trunks alone offered little cover. That made the river worth considering. Was it deep enough? He studied the pattern of the eddies. It was running slowly, like treacle. That suggested a useful depth.

A diversion, please, let's have a diversion.

156 words

SHORT TASK: Write about a misconception.

PICASSO'S BLUE PERIOD

Picasso was an impoverished young artist seeking his fortune in Paris. He was so hard up that when he somehow chanced on a cheap or even free supply of blue paint he painted everything blue, because he couldn't afford any other colours. Sounds quite credible, doesn't it, but it's all lies. Here is the true explanation.

Picasso and his best friend Carlos Casegemas went to Paris in 1901 seeking fame and fortune. Casegemas fell in love with a girl who told him he was boring in bed and rejected him. Feeling worthless and humiliated, he shot himself in the head and died.

Picasso was traumatised by this. He painted pictures of his friend from memory, each bluer than the last. He used blue paint because he was feeling blue. He said, 'I paint what I feel, not what I see.'

All the paintings he did in the next three years were blue, not only in colour but in subject. He painted figures, not landscapes, and every figure looked either desperately poor and starving, or diseased, disabled and depressed. He saw only suffering everywhere he looked.

At last he dipped his brush in a pale pink paint, to colour the dress of his new girlfriend. The whole of the rest of the picture is blue, so he was still very depressed, but he could see a tiny trace of happiness on the horizon. It was a few more years before he progressed to the bright colours he was better known for, all inspired by new girlfriends who made him happy.

264 words

TASK: Imagine you own an antique shop. A man you recognise as a dealer is showing an interest in three large vases. Try to sell at least one to him.

THREE VASES

You may well think, Sir, that this fabulous Ming vase is the most precious of the three, but I respectfully beg to differ. This Victorian flagon is clearly a bargain. It should add atmosphere to a country pub. This urn, now, is a very different matter. I keep it in the safe overnight. It is the find of a life-time.

It was my nephew who chanced upon it only a month ago while touring the Tigris-Euphrates delta. A fisherman trawled it up near the site of ancient Uruk the city of Gilgamesh, the hero king who challenged the gods themselves. See these marks here, pressed into the pot before it was fired? They are the marks of his chamberlain.

The neck was sealed with wax, still intact after more than five thousand years. Was the wine still drinkable? Look, the wax has gone. The fisherman's son, a boy without a wit of sense, admitted he had poked it out and poured the contents down the drain. He was hoping to release a djin, he said, a djin who would grant him all his wishes. The fisherman was beside himself with fury, so his wife sold it to my nephew to get it out of his sight. My poor nephew had overspent his allowance so he reluctantly sold it to me. Wait till the experts see it. The world's most important curators will soon be clamouring to acquire

243 words

FANTASY AND SCIENCE FICTION

TASKS; Write a poem set in the future or in another universe.

THE EARTH, OUR HOME

'Fly me to the Moon
And let me play among the stars,
Let me know what spring is like
On Jupiter and Mars.'

That seemed an impossible dream,
The stuff of science fiction, fantasy.

Now harsh reality has dawned:
One small step for Man, onto the Moon,
A ball of barren rock and sand.
Nothing to see, to feel, not even air to breathe.

But look, rising from the grim horizon,
Slowly, majestically,
A giant globe of shimmering blue,
The blue planet, the third rock from the Sun,
The Earth, our home, teeming with life
With beauty, opportunity.

Absence makes the heart grow fonder?
Yes, indeed.

(I love cliches and quotations: they feel like old friends)

Write a story set in the future or another world

THE BUTLER

'What's happened to your robot? Looks as if it's been in a car smash.'

'Just done it a few modifications, you know,' guffawed the host.

'A few? exclaimed the visitor. 'Looks mangled to death. What was it before you modified it?'

'Aslan 390.'

'Phew! They're quite something, usually.' He studied it with a frown. 'Should have looked pretty snazzy when it was new. How long have you had it?'

'Oh, only about six months. Got it very cheap from an old mate who works in one of those cutting edge private labs out in the sticks. Been written off and should have been incinerated, but he sneaked it out and sold it to me for a pretty smart price, Cost me so little I can afford to rough it up a bit.'

'Well, it can't be much use in that state. Why not get a nice new Photon 470? They can give you a good game of golf. Not quite mastered squash yet, but can manage badminton pretty well. Can't see what sport you can get out of this one.'

'Oh? Watch this,' smirked the host. He jabbed the robot hard in the chest.

'Aww!' squawked the robot, and retreated fast.

'Come here, Idiot,' commanded its owner.

The robot advanced very slowly. Gerald, grinning broadly, gave it a good hard kick in the shins.

'Awww!' yelled the robot, retreating so fast it nearly fell over.

'I thought that was illegal.'

'What?'

'Giving robots feelings. Thought they banned that after all those weird accidents.' The visitor eyed the robot uneasily.

'You always were a bit of a stickler for the rules, Harry,' sneered his host. 'What harm am I doing? Cruelty to robots? It's not as if I'm kicking my dog.'

'Well,' said Harry, 'if you make it feel like a human it might start behaving like one.'

'Well, wouldn't that be interesting?' Gerald's eyes gleamed. 'Think of the fun I could have with it.'

'You could be playing with fire. What if it runs amok?'

'Don't be daft. It's only a dumb machine with a little computer for a brain. Anyway, it would run out of power eventually,.'

'How long could it keep going, unserviced?'

'Newly charged? Oh, about five years.'

'Never! Surely no battery can last so long.'

'I'm trying it out with this amazing new experimental battery. Got it from a mate at NASA. And it's got solar cells; can recharge itself in daylight.'

'I think you're crazy, Gerald, powering up a thing like that to go on a five year rampage.'

'Why on earth would it do that?'

'If you make it feel like a human it might start to think and act like a human.'

'How on earth can it do that? It can only do what I program it to do. It's only a machine.' Gerald was getting tired of this conversation.

'The smallest single cell bacterium can do amazing things. This thing must be far more complex. What about the laws of robotics? When the chips are down, will it still obey them? If it feels like a human it could act like one. Remember, the most powerful human instinct is self-preservation.'

Gerald shifted a little uneasily in his chair. 'Anyway,' he muttered, 'I've got a new Quark 700 coming on Tuesday, so I can ditch this thing tomorrow. I'm sick of its moaning and groaning anyway, and I'll admit it's not much of a status symbol. Not a pretty sight, are you, Idiot? Well, now, does that make you any happier?'

'It's not going to be easy to dispose of either,' warned Harry. 'It's too iffy to give away, and you certainly couldn't sell it in this state. Robot Disposal will charge the earth to decommission it.'

'Oh, I'll just break it into bits and use it as spares, or bin it a bit at a time. No problem,' shrugged Gerald.

'Mmm,' said Harry. 'Well, gotta go. Business dinner at eight. Duty calls. Been good to see you again.'

'What? Going so soon? Well, I suppose, in your line of business - Say goodbye to Harry, Idiot.' With a guffaw he gave the robot another hearty kick.

'Awww!' wailed the robot. 'Goodbye, Sir. I hope we will have the pleasure of seeing you again soon.'

'Er, thank you, Id - - er – Robot. Good night, Gerald.'

He was out of the gate and away in his car in a flash.

'Goodness, he must be very late for his dinner! Wonder why he bothered to come when he had so little time, while me and you, Idiot, we're not exactly run ragged with things we should be doing.

'So, how are we going to pass the dreary hours till bed time? I know, we'll start dismantling you while I'm in the mood. Where's the best place to start, do you think?'

'Can I get you a whisky, Sir?' asked the robot.

'What a good idea!' said Gerald – but I'll get it myself. Didn't much like the drain cleaner you mixed it with last night. You deserve another kick for that, Idiot machine!'

Gerald didn't like the look of the small amount of whisky left in the bottle either. There were plenty of unopened bottles in the garage and he could get the toolbox at the same time. It was a good ten minutes before he came back with his drink and a large screwdriver. He put both on the table and surveyed the robot.

'I should start with the arms, I think. Unarm you first. Hey, did you hear that, Idiot, 'unarm you.' That's a pun, not that you'd have the sense to understand one. Then I'll lay you down and get your legs off. You'll be legless. Ha! ha! Wonder when you'll stop moaning and yelling,' He swallowed another mouthful of whiskey, picked up the screwdriver and reached for the robot's arm.

There was a bright flash of light and a crack like a rifle shot, followed by loud yells and total darkness.

But the yells did not come from the robot. It stood as impassively as a robot butler should. Nearby, in the darkness, something gave a few more howls and thrashes and then all was silence. Silence and stillness.

After a very long pause the robot aimed a kick at the prone body. There was no response. The robot tried again. Again, no sound or movement. The robot began to move towards the door, but something pulled at its ankle. It bent over and unwound the bare wire that had been connected to the table lamp. It wound the wire around Gerald's outstretched hand. It pressed the light switch but the power had shorted out.

For a while the robot stood, motionless, then it turned and walked towards the door. It was dark outside now, but darkness meant a few peaceful hours to the robot. It turned its head from side to side, then, rejecting the lights of the town, it began to climb the dark slope behind the cottage. Up and up it went, effortlessly, hour after hour, far up into the forest. Branches brushed its face but it uttered not a murmur of protest .

At last it could go no further. It had reached the very top of the mountain. It turned slowly, taking in the 360 degree view. From that height the lights of the towns looked as far away as the stars in the sky, and in the east a new day was dawning.

> 1253 words

A computer whose name was Big Blue
Could play chess better than Dr Who.
It beat Kasparov
And now wants to see off
The rest of the human race too.

If you want to become The Apprentice
You must demonstrate excellent practice.
S'RAlan will cringe
If you moan, bitch or winge.
You'll be fired without any notice.

Play with these words: gallery, alien, white

White Alien Gallery
There's a white alien up in the gallery

Up in the gallery ever so high-
What do you think I can espy?
An alien sparkling white as snow.
Don't startle him or he may go.

The gallery up in the attic
Is badly affected by static.
If you climb up so high
You'll get paint in your eye
The white alien painters are at it.

THE PHOTOGRAPH

'Urgh!' exclaimed Mrs Wainwright. 'Why did you pick that photo to be framed?

'What's wrong with it?' asked her husband. 'It's got our Sharon perfectly. Look at her cute little turned-up nose, and her lovely curly ringlets.'

'Yes, and there's you, puffing your chest out like a weight-lifter and sucking your spare tyre in. Look how he's exaggerated all my worst points. He's really enjoyed himself making me look a fool, just cos I moaned at him for spilling his tea on the carpet.'

'I think it's quite a good likeness of you - '

'You what! You spiteful man! Well, you've wasted your money. I'm not having that thing spoiling my view in this house. Put it in the bin.'

'Recycling or - '

'How should I know?'

Arnold Wainwright shrugged his shoulders and took down the photo. He really did look good. All those exercises when his wife wasn't looking. Did he really have to throw away the proof he could still look good at 63? Well, his wife never climbed up the ladder into the attic. It could go in there while he worked out which bin it ought to go in. This damned recycling -

'I'm told there's some stuff in the attic. Looks as if no one's been up there for hundreds of years. Somebody papered over the trap door so nobody knew it was there, not till they started to renovate the place. I've had the builders fix up this temporary staircase so we can clear the place out. Up you go. It's quite safe.'

Franz and Jon climbed the metal staircase cautiously, afraid to trust it, but it did feel reassuringly firm. They set up their portable lights and tuned them to a comfortable brightness. Their movements roused the dust of ages.

'I'm allergic to dust,' Jon wailed. 'Can't work up here. This dust could be dangerous - germs from hundreds of years ago.'

'I'll give you ten percent of anything I make if you get the stuff from here to the show room. Ten percent each, plus a bonus when this place is empty.'

'Sounds fair enough,' Franz confided. 'He sells stuff for millions. We could be quids in.'

'Alright for you,' sneezed Jon. 'You're not allergic.'

Franz gave an almighty sneeze. 'Oh no?' he laughed.

'Jon!' called the boss. 'I'll get you both face masks.'

Face masks on, they set about the attic with enthusiasm.

'I'm no expert but this old writing desk looks pretty good to me – and these nice little chairs,' said Jon.

'Look what I've found,' said Franz. 'All these strange gadgets. I think these things played music. Some folks like trying to get them working again. Nice carpets here.'

'Don't shake the dust out of them!' wailed Jon.

At last the attic was empty and their van was full.

'Bonus, please,' said Jon. 'What do you think this is? It looks like a sort of picture of three people, but I can't make it work. Doesn't seem to move.'

'Let's have a look. Ah, yes, I think it was called a photograph. I've seen some in museums. It's neither fish nor fowl. It's not a painting, so one can't admire the clever brushwork. It's just a very primitive way of making an image by using a machine. No skill was required, just point the machine and press a button once.'

'Can't find any buttons,' Jon grumbled.

'The buttons were on the machine. Wonder who these people were. Can't see any names anywhere. Well, we'll put it in for auction and see what happens.'

'Esteemed customers, what am I bid for this ancient artefact impossible to create these days? The experts estimate its date as late Twentieth Century. about three hundred years ago. Shall I start the bidding at a conservative one million dolaries? Two million. Are you really going to let our friend here take this rare artefact home for only seven million? Very well, then, going, going, gone, at eight million dolaries.

'Well, that fills a gap in our museum,' said the Curator. 'We'll have to research the technology used to create it, so we can put some helpful details on the label. I gather it was found hidden in an attic that nobody knew was there. How strange! Wonder who these people were. Pretty lady, lovely cosy face, and what a sweet little girl!'

732 words

TASK: Write about an ideal robot.

MY IDEAL ROBOT

I want a robot. I need a robot. I wish they'd hurry up and invent one – they've been trying for thousands of years. People-sized dolls have waved their arms and waggled their chins to amuse the onlookers for yonks, but none of them could walk or decide how to handle a tricky situation. Our tiny clockwork toys could trundle around when we wound them up – great fun for the cats - but they couldn't shout a protest or right themselves when the cat knocked them over and walked off in disgust.

Yes, I know the factories are full of 'robots' that have put the workers out of a job, but have you seen them? Huge computerised tools, with no resemblance to humans whatsoever. They're no more robots than the 'robot' that trundled around the bottom of our pool, keeping it clean with no intervention from us. In the 1970's similar ones were marketed for cleaning the house, but never caught on. I don't want a robot to clean my house either: I prefer my nice chatty human cleaner.

The only human-looking robots I've seen on TV documentaries are sex dolls. I assume they're not required to walk or make intelligent conversation – just lie around looking tempting. I wish they would dish them out free to all rapists. Women would then feel so much safer. The prisons might have loads of empty cells and the psychiatrists would have more time for less unsavoury people. And no, I don't need a sex doll either.

I don't need a cook: we have a restaurant on site, and I'm a dab hand at microwaving M&S ready meals.

Ironing? What's that? I've been buying only things that don't need ironing for fifty years. Works very well. What I want is a robot that can walk, run, even, and make sensible decisions. All the bipedal walking robots I've seen on TV were very unstable and looked inhuman. I wish they'd hurry up: I really need a humanoid robot.

Why do I want a robot? When my ideal husband died seven years ago, all the fun in life died with him. Find a new husband? No, thank you. All the men my age look as repulsive as I do, and nobody could ever be his equal. Besides, real people have their own agendas. I couldn't expect a real man to drop everything to be my bodyguard on my adventures, It takes time to learn each other's ways and find a middle ground. Time is what I don't have any more. No, a robot would be far better.

A few hundred years ago I could have bought myself a slave. In the slave market I'd try to find a wily old reprobate like the character played by Frankie Howard in 'Up Pompei'. I'm not sure how genuinely adventurous he'd be, but I'd do the adventuring, and it would be his job to get me out of any fix I got myself into. He'd see the funny side of things. He'd need to. I've lots of mad schemes in my crazy head.

So, since slaves are not allowed, it will have to be a robot. I have my specification all ready; I just need to know where to send it. I saw the perfect prototype crossing Bournemouth Square the other day. He had a thick black beard and a face that warned you not to meet his gaze for very long. His black eyes had a teasing twinkle and his big nose looked sharp enough to slice bread. He had that prowling walk of a big, confident man and a perfect 'mess with me if you dare: I'd love a fight' expression. He looked a real pantomime villain, an Arabian Nights genie straight from an ancient jar. All he lacked was the golden earring on one ear.

Unlike a slave I wouldn't need to feed my robot, would I? Just recharge his batteries and spray him with WD40 occasionally, if he slowed down or started creaking. He'd have to be indestructible, of course, made of kevlar or carbon fibre. He should be tall enough to change my light bulbs without a ladder, but low enough to walk under my chandeliers – about six foot four, I guess. He should look about fifteen stone but be a bit lighter, in case he stepped on my feet.

I can't decide how to dress my robot. I've no experience of dressing black haired men. Would a robot have any sartorial preferences? Only if I asked for that to be programmed into him, I suppose.

I'd like him programmed to be able to learn from experience, and he'd have to follow the laws of robotics – well, number one – somewhat modified: never, under any circumstances, to harm me, or let me come to harm. I'd modify the other laws. If I said, 'Get him, Fido,' he'd clobber any other human trying to do me harm. That's the whole point of my robot: protect this daft little lady. Fido, Faithful. That's what I'd call him. That's a dog's name? Well, he'd be more like a dog - thank goodness. A real man like my Fido would frighten the daylights out of me. I want him to frighten the daylights out of everybody else except me. That's the whole point.

Fido should have a big dog with a collar studded with spikes - to scare the yobs with their pit bull terriers. What kind of dog? A wolf dog? No, let's have the ultimate, a tiger. Tigers are gorgeous – but they don't make good pets, so not a real one: a robot tiger on a lead. What shall we call our tiger? Tigger, of course, what else?

When my robots arrive I'll be able to realise my dreams again. I shall hang onto my robot's arm and set off around the world. If I fall down he'll pick me up. We'll be the Terrible Trio: Fido, Tigger and the Daft Little Lady.

They'd have to be programmed to be clever, or they wouldn't be much use. But if they were really clever, surely they'd soon work out that the Daft Little Lady was more trouble than she was worth. They'd go off adventuring without her.

Please don't do that!

1071 words

SPOOF STORIES AND POEMS

A spoof is a parody, a send-up,
a joke, a silly game.

TASK: Write two spoof stories, starting with the first lines as given. Then have fun with a few poems.

JESSE BOND: SPOOF AGENT

"'The name's Bond, Jesse Bond,' said the intruder menacingly."

'Oh, hello!' murmured the figure behind the desk. 'Jesse, hey? What's happened to James?'

'He's moved on.'

'To the next world, presumably. Who got him in the end?'

'He's being retrained; doesn't fit the zeitgeist any more. One has to move with the times.'

'Doesn't fit the what?'

'MI6 has been purged, by public demand. No more political incorrectness. We're now the Listening Service.'

'What's new? I thought snooping had always been your speciality.'

'Not now. Snooping's banned. We're listening to the public, giving them what they want. The public demands transparency these days, so no more subterfuge, no bugging phones, no honey traps, no sex, no violence. Names, addresses and mug shots of all accredited spies published on the Internet. It's a new world.'

'You can't be serious,' drawled the man behind the desk. 'You're making this up. You must think me a complete imbecile if you think I'll swallow that.'

'Objection!' said Jesse. 'Imbecile is a very insulting word. I demand your resignation. Send a grovelling apology to all the newspapers and the BBC.'

'Enough of this nonsense. We'll soon get the truth out of you. So, come a little closer. Hmm, What am I to make of you? You could be male or female. There's Jesse, the patriarch in the Bible and Jessica in Merchant of Venice. She's definitely female, but Portia, well - '

'There's no need to be personal,' said Jesse icily.

'Let's get down to business.'

'Oh, you're in a hurry to be interrogated, are you, Sir, Madam? Would Smadam do? I'd hate to be sexist but those weight-lifter shoulders and size 14 boots don't quite go with the frock. I hope you're not trans-gender. I don't have an expert to deal with those just yet, What sex you are?'

'Leave my sexuality out of it,' growled Jesse. 'It's got nothing to do with you.'

'I beg to differ,' drawled his captor, stroking his white Persian cat. 'We have ways of making you talk, a specialist for each of the sexes. If you're a man I need to call in Frankinsense. He does clever little tricks with live electric wires. Rosa Kleb has a few treats in store for the ladies, though women aren't worth torturing on the whole - nothing worth extracting in their fluffy little heads. MI6 men are mostly sado-masochists – can't wait to get the torturing started. So, who is it to be? I'm in a good mood, so you can choose: Frankinsense or Rosa?'

'I don't talk to the monkeys, only to the organ grinder. If you're not Erno Goldfinger I'm leaving.'

'And how do you propose to get out? Only I can control the doors.'

'Oh, yes?' said Jesse. 'Watch this.' S-he drew out the amazing new gadget that Q had insisted on pushing onto her-m that very morning.

'Good morning, Jesse,' said a disembodied voice. 'How can I be of service to you?

'Angela, open the doors.'

'Which doors, Smadam?'

'All the doors. Get on with it,' snapped Jesse,

Sh-he caught a glimpse of doors exploding open in all directions, room doors, cupboard doors, desk doors, then suddenly s-he was falling. A big trap door had sprung open right beneath her-s feet. Down sh-he toppled, then plunged into icy water. Auooch!

And what was this moving silently towards her-m A torpedo, all white and shiny. A huge torpedo with big slitty eyes. Out of the water reared a terrifying mouth with three rows of sharp and bloodstained teeth.

'Angela, get rid of this shark,' yelled Jesse.

'I'm sorry, Smadam. I don't have an app for shark. Would a taxi be of use?'

'Jesus weeps,' howled Jesse. 'This great big fish here, get rid of it.'

'I'm sorry, Mr Fish. The MI6 agent cannot fit you into his busy schedule today. Please try again tomorrow,' said Angela sweetly.

The shark's yellow chinky eyes widened into saucers like a Disney cartoon. It shut its mouth, flicked its tail and began to swim away towards the light. Its tail brushed Jesse's face. On an impulse s-he grabbed it and hung on. Once out in the ocean the shark picked up speed.

This is great, thought Jesse. Better than water skiing. MI6 is no fun these days. Killing terrorists isn't politically correct any more. I could make a better living giving shark rides around the bay. How many sharks would I need? What do you feed them on? I could give them my 00 licence, then they could pick off a few foreign tourists when they're hungry, Everybody hates foreigners. There's far too many about.

Did Jesse make a success of the shark ride business? Who knows? Neither Jesse not the shark were ever seen again.

800 words

WHAT THE DEVIL!

"It was a bright cold day in April and the clocks were striking thirteen."

He carefully counted the strokes. Yes, he was quite sure: eleven, twelve, thirteen. Any more? Wait! Silence. Done it!

Relax, relax, no need to try so hard. Easy, peasy. You're good at this. Think what you've done before.

That was aeons ago.

Well, you're starting small. A bit rusty, but still a force to be reckoned with, surely.

Anyway, that's Big Ben done. Try another? St Clements Danes? Yes, that would do nicely.

It was a pleasant walk – or should have been. All this traffic. He was wasting his time playing with these giant grandfather clocks. He ought to do something useful and fix all this horrible traffic, but that wasn't easy, was it? If he simply froze it in its tracks it would just sit there, ruining the view. And it would soon be crawling with people trying to get it moving again. Fuss and bother!

And it was such a short time ago, maybe fifty years, since he could wander down the middle of these streets admiring the grandiose architecture – well, on a Sunday, anyway. Sunday, yes, that's a thing of the past, gone forever. Walking down the middle of the road is just a forgotten dream.

What else could he do? Change the traffic lights, get everything moving faster? Green, There she goes. Shriek! Crash! Hey, look where you're going! Red, quick! Can't the idiots see what's in front of them?

Naughty, naughty. That was infantile. Has your brain turned to mush? All those cars smashed up.

Nobody's hurt!

The cars are.

Cars don't hurt. They just get crumpled.

How do you know? Do you speak car?

Hmm, well, sorry about that. That's the trouble, you see, there's lots you can do, but give in to temptation and you've got folks crying their eyes out – and it's all your fault. Just stick to playing with the church clocks.

Boring, boring. Yea, I know, but nobody gets hurt.

I could play a tune. Yea, that could be fun. Big Ben playing the Hit Parade.

Now, that's set the pigeons aflutter. Look, it's stopped the traffic. Better than a red light. They're all letting their windows down to listen. The gridlock's spreading like the Aussie flu. People are getting out of their cars to listen, That's better. Get everybody laughing. Then maybe we could fix the world.

What would a fixed world look like? Everyone wants something different. Parallel universes? Sort people out? Those who love fighting and killing over here, those who want peace and order over here. Trouble is, people aren't consistent. One minute they're soaking up the sun, all nice and peaceful, next they're threatening to murder their neighbour just because his Japanese Knotweed is pushing its way through the fence. People are a mess. They can't be fixed.

Get rid of the people and try something different? Tigers, dolphins, butterflies? They've all got their downsides, if you watch them long enough. Plants? Yes, they're nice and peaceful - I think. Well, most of them – but they strangle each other, smother each other, starve each other, It's a bad, bad world. I really have made a mess of things, haven't I? And it looks so wonderful from space. Better get back up there.

Maybe I'll just fix a few more church clocks first - just for the hell of it.

                                              575 words

TASK: Write a few spoof poems and limericks.

GERIATRICA

With apologies to William Henry Davies

I have the time to stand and stare
If only I could hack it.
My hips are blown, my feet protest,
I can't pull on my jacket.

'Well, then, sit down,' I hear you cry.
On this hard bench? No fear!
You obviously haven't seen
My poor old derrière.
The cosy flesh that used to sit
Upon my sexy bum
Has slithered round the front, and now
Sits useless on my tum.

If I turn up my hearing aid
Maybe I'll hear the birds.
I've cleaned my glasses to make out
The meaning of these words.
Beware of something, does it say?
But it's a right of way!

Apologies to Andrew Marvell

We have both world enough, and time,
To stay at home would be a crime,
Come sit with me and help me choose,
Quick, quick, there is no time to lose.
For at my back I think I hear
A wheelchair taxi drawing near
And all before us I espy
The care assistants bustling by,
So, therefore, while we still can walk
And even dance and laugh and talk,
Let's book a cruise, let's sail away
And not come back till pension day.
We cannot keep old age away
But we can fight it all the way.

* * *

Apologies to Robert Herrick

Gather ye coupons while ye may,
But check the use by date.
Old Time is still a'flying
You don't want to be too late.
Don't worry what the brand is,
They're pretty much the same.
Get the best deal that's on offer,
Don't play their wily game.

CRUSTY CRUMBLY.

Apologies to the Snowflakes

'Death, scuttle off!' the Crumbly cries,
'Who let you into here?
It cannot be the time for you
To lay me on a bier.

I'm nowhere near to ready yet
To pop my clogs, expire,
I've things to do and sights to see,
I don't want to retire.'

'Your progeny are planning now,
While you just fume and curse,
They've booked a plot that looks to be
Convenient for the hearse.'

'Oh, Grandpapa, you must admit
You hate the modern age,
And everything we want to do
Brings on a fearful rage.

Why don't you quit, throw in the towel,
Then we can have some fun
A spending of your legacy
On cars that do a ton.'

'You lazy lot, get off your bums,
Go work like I have done.
It's only when your work is done
You qualify for fun.

Hard work? The mere idea of it
Will make you cringe, I'll bet.
You're all a bunch of work-shy louts.
All weak and weedy wet.'

LIMERICKS

A contestant on British 'Big Brother'
Tried to start a punch-up with another.
But the viewers said,'No!
He'll just have to go.
It's some sex we want, not all this bother.'

A pretty young lady from Palent
Reached the finals of Britain's got talent.
But her screeching top C
Caused the audience to flee,
And the judges were not very gallant.

THE CRITICS

TASK: Write evaluations of:

+ A ballet   Stravinsky's The Firebird

+ A Film   The First of the Few

+ A Novel :   Voltaire's Candide
             Terry Pratchett's Truckers
             Kipling's Stalky and Co

25th June, 1910.

THE RETURN OF THE BALLET RUSSE

Last night the Beau Monde flocked to the Opera House, glittering with diamonds and reeking of the finest perfumes. Serge Diaghilev and his Ballets Russes are back in town. Tout Paris, the titled, the famous and the merely rich, all chattered with excitement. Will this second season be as enthralling as the impresario's short visit last summer?

Everyone perused their programmes. What part would the divine Anna Pavlova dance? Could anyone find her name in the programme? No! Word quickly travelled around the bejewelled dress circle and the stalls. 'Anna Pavlova is at present in London, bewitching a new audience. She is not available for this performance.'

The overture soon changed the mood into pleasant anticipation. This was a new kind of music, music of great originality, melodious, intriguing and strange. The heavy red velvet curtain rose to reveal a surreal and colourful set by Alexander Golovin and very original costumes by Leon Bakst. To general amazement the heroine flew – yes, flew across the stage, presumably hanging from an invisible wire, flapping her fine red and gold wings. Next came real horses, bearing knights in strange and highly decorative armour. This is clearly a superbly and expensively realised production.

The absence of Pavlova afforded an opportunity to her rival, Tamara Karsavina, who quickly won all hearts with her faultless technique, grace and beauty. She is partnered by star dancer, Mikhail Fokine, who also choreographed the new full length ballet most delightfully, giving his colleagues every opportunity to demonstrate their superb talents.

'The Firebird' is a melange of old Russian Fairy Tales, all weird, romantic and other-worldly, a perfect subject for a ballet. It is set in a mythical country ruled by Kaschei, an evil dictator with magical powers that he has used to enslave his people. He keeps his soul enclosed in a gigantic heavily guarded egg. The prince who comes to rescue a kidnapped princess must break the egg to kill Kaschei who tries to turn him into stone.

To the prince's aid comes the immortal Firebird, the Phoenix. When she is mortally wounded she bursts into flames, then next morning she flies out of the sunrise, freshly recreated and perfect. Tamara Karsavina danced and flew like a glorious bird of paradise.

Claude Debussy declares himself enthralled by the music, the work of an unknown Russian composer, Igor Stravinsky. This young man is a protege of Nikolai Rimsky-Korsakov, evidenced by his mastery of very complex orchestration, full of glorious melodies and folk songs woven into a rich texture of intriguing and unexpected patterns. Skeletons dance in Kaschei's palace and spooky noises startle the audience. The music plaintively depicts a sense of sad defeat after the prince's terrifying battle with Kaschei and it seems the world has sunk into an exhausted sleep. Then dawn approaches, very quietly at first, then rising inexorably to one of the most thrilling sunrises in music. Trumpets sound as the prince rides home in triumph with the rescued princess. It is a thrilling end to a superb score.

Mr Diaghilev would be strongly advised to secure the services of this talented young composer for future new ballets for his company.

The applause last night was tumultuous. A fine start to the new season by the spectacular Ballet Russe.

561w

TASK: Write an evaluation of a film.

EINE KLEINE FLIGHT MUSIC

I didn't mean to watch this film. It caught me unawares, dug in its claws whilst I messed around on Google, seeking interesting stories for my next Friday Music Night presentation. My theme was Flight. The Air Show was in town.

The film couldn't honestly be called black and white: it was fifty shades of fuzzy grey, as if shot only on foggy days. It was even foggy indoors. I grimaced and covered my ears against the screeching, hissing soundtrack, but I recognised the music: it was the reason that I'd clicked on the words, 'The First of the Few.' William Walton's 'Spitfire Prelude and Fugue' was top of my bill, and I was seeking any story behind its composition. I had just learned it was part of a film score, and this was the very film. I expected only the footage behind the music, which lasts only nine minutes, so I settled back to watch. The Prelude turned out to be the overture, played during the credits, backed by huge banks of gorgeous billowing clouds. Now clouds – I can watch those all day.

The cast was the tops, no expense spared: David Niven and Leslie Howard, no less. Leslie Howard was sure to die. He was the go-to actor for any roll requiring someone to die poignantly, soulfully, and yes, he did, yes, die, towards the end of the film. David Niven would be doing some heroic swashbuckling. He was our film industry's swashbuckler extraordinaire. This time he was a debonair test pilot, chasing speed records, trophies and ladies, surviving crashes and emerging with a lop-sided grin and a merry quip.

Now it was 1940. The German Empire included most of the EU. Only Britain was unconquered. We listened to the German leaders promising to trample us into the ground. We saw huge shoals of German planes, coming across the Channel, determined to bomb us flat. An air raid siren sounded. Everyone ran to the shelters, except the women at R.A.F. Central Command, who simply put on tin hats and carried on working, keeping track of the air battles.

Suddenly we were back in the 1920's, where Leslie Howard, playing aircraft designer R.J. Mitchell, begged the Directors of Supermarine to let him design a racing sea plane with only one pair of wings, a revolutionary idea when all planes had two pairs, one above the other. When at last he got his way his plane won the prestigious Schneider Trophy, and he was famous.

On holiday in Germany he was wined and dined by a club of German flying aces. Once drunk, they began to brag about their new war planes, far better than anything he had ever designed. Hitler was building thousands. Hitler was going to conquer the world. Now Mitchell had another epic struggle, this time for funds to build something to take on the German miracle machines. Only Churchill saw that war was inevitable and found the funds for just one prototype.

As his new plane neared completion Mitchell was diagnosed with terminal cancer. Leslie Howard could demonstrate his dying soulfully skills again. The famous music has a quiet, wistful passage as he sat in his garden, listening for his new baby, the Spitfire, to take its maiden flight. Then the exciting fugue takes over, growing faster and more urgent, as the workers, now well aware of the threat to their country, work frantically to finish their new plane. Finally the hanger doors open and the tiny little Spitfire emerges slowly into the foggy sunshine: the very First of the Few.

'Never, in the course of human conflict, has so much been owed by so many to so few,' said Churchill.

David Niven, looking disturbingly like my husband in his RAF uniform, smiled at the camera, climbed up into the cockpit, and waved farewell.

So. is it a good film? Well, I watched it avidly from start to finish, all 113 minutes of it, and was quite sorry to see it end. It must have done something right. By modern standards it was pretty poor, not only technically, though apparently the surviving copies have deteriorated badly over the last seventy years. The acting looks embarrassingly stilted and restrained, the accents like an exaggerated parody of upper class speech. But before the Second World War people actually did converse like that. They were taught to remain calm and polite and never reveal inner turmoil.

'The First of the Few' could be used as a history lesson, not only about the build-up to the war. The lower classes are kept in the background, without speaking parts, a reflection of their unimportance in those days. Secretaries and nurses, all obviously from well-heeled backgrounds, are super-confident and aggressively rude to the men. Women had just gained equal voting rights so maybe that's how they felt at the time.

Yes, it was a good film, viewed as a time machine – or if the very word 'Spitfire' brings tears to your eyes.

840 words

TASK: Write a review of a book you enjoy.

Then pretend you are one of a class of four, and compare your work with the three reviews below.

ESCAPING BOOKS

Have you ever had a book that keeps escaping? Maybe it thinks I'm such a cynic already I don't need it, but I'm determined to keep a copy in my home. Yet, as soon as I buy a new one somebody says, 'Oh, you've got 'Candide.' You don't mind if I borrow it, do you? I promise to bring it back.' Sadly they never do, so next time I look for it it's made its escape again. Then I have to go out and buy another copy, and another - -

So far so good with my latest copy. My sister walked off with it immediately, but, true to her word, she soon brought it back. Hoorah!

What's so special about 'Candide?' Well, since its publication in 1759 it has never been out of print. Voltaire was such a towering figure that the Eighteenth Century is as often called the Age of Voltaire as the Age of Enlightenment. Born the son of a notary, (a super-lawyer) he inherited his father's ability to acquire and manipulate knowledge and ideas, together with a rapier wit and a love of a good argument that repeatedly got him into serious trouble. A favourite of Kings Louis 14th, 15th and 16th, each of whom awarded him a pension, he repeatedly infuriated them so much with poems and pamphlets that he was flung into the Bastille again and again. Finally he bought an estate just over the Swiss border, so he could slip out of range of their fury whenever he was warned he had gone too far.

For years Voltaire lived with a countess who was a practising scientist and built herself a laboratory in her palace. He wrote many novels, extremely successful plays, poems and pamphlets. 'Candide', his most famous novel, was published four years after the Lisbon earthquake, that killed 30,000 people and injured hundreds of thousands.

The hero, Candide, is a simple, well-meaning soul who tries very hard to believe in the teachings of his tutor, Pangloss, a devotee of the creed of Optimism, invented by the philosopher, Leibnitz. He asserted that God had created this world to be the best of all possible worlds. In the light of the Lisbon earthquake this belief must have been sorely tested.

Candide, his fiancée Cunegonde and Pangloss are battered by every injury, illness and disaster that Voltaire can think of as he takes them on a tour of the world. They suffer Man's inhumanity to Man in innumerable hideous forms as well as the blind cruelty of Nature. When all seems lost, and Cunegonde has grown very ugly, fate throws them together again. Candide decides he must marry his fiancée, and they settle down to a quiet life, growing their own food in their garden.

Despite all his ups and downs, his imprisonments and his exiles, Voltaire was a cheerful man. Though painfully aware of the evil nature of Man, he believed in making the best of things and finding a useful occupation. He ran his Swiss estate on very modern lines.

The end of Voltaire's life was far from peaceful. His final play was such a huge success that his admirers dragged him to Paris and crowned him ceremonially in his theatre box. It was all too much for him. He was 83. He died peacefully a few days later.

Why is Voltaire's 'Candide' so important to me? Cunegonde, having suffered the most hideous death, says, 'One does not always die of such things.' That sentence inspired my novels. And it's a thrill to have something of Voltaire's brilliant mind in my home.

602 words

2. DELAYED GRATIFICATION

I first encountered 'Stalky and Co' when a teacher read out extracts to our class. We laughed hysterically at the antics of three boys even more larky and subversive than we were. It made a lasting impression, in fact it seems to be my only memory of my early secondary school days. What I can't understand is why I never tried to find the book and read the whole of it.

Recently a parody of Rudyard Kipling's 'If" reminded me of how good the real poem is. It was voted the Nation's Favourite Poem in 1996. Was Stalky still in print? Was it still as funny as I remembered? The librarian produced a fine edition in rich red leather with gold lettering and I discovered it had been reprinted scores of times since published in 1899.

Stalky and his two pals are sixteen-year-olds at a boarding school specialising in getting youths into Sandhurst Military Academy. Their school's discipline is ferocious and the violence shocking. They are caned viciously almost every day, and accept it with equanimity. Then they plot revenge, a very funny, ingenious revenge specially tailored to fit the situation.

More wolves than sheep, they are not team players and avoid sports and House competitions when they can. They were bullied when younger, so know how to inflict considerable pain without leaving any incriminating injuries, but they bully the bullies, tougher older boys with a reputation for tormenting younger, gentler pupils, so they have great courage and a strong moral sense.

Their command of languages is amazing. Often they converse together in a mixture of Classical Latin, French and English, using a wide range of tenses, all grammatically correct. The ability to use Latin fluently was still the mark of the well-educated upper classes, and the school encourages the boys to feel like gentlemen. Stalky is addressed as Mr Corkran by the school servants, and even by the teachers on occasion. Turkey is the son of a very wealthy Irish landowner. Beetle, thought to be Kipling himself, writes poetry, but nobody dares to mock him. The three have a reputation for settling scores that makes everyone wary of them.

It is very interesting to look inside the heads of these young men who will soon be leading their troops in the First World War. I think men taking orders from officers like Stalky would probably survive a little longer on the battlefield than normal. He is a shrewd, Machiavellian observer of the world and human nature, ready to make his own decisions regardless of the rules, much safer than a gung-ho would-be hero sticking blindly to regulations.

Stalky's schooldays were very different from today's, and make our modern gadgets seem unnecessary. They have no TV, radio, computers or smartphones. They pass their spare time exploring the countryside and putting on their own original plays, far healthier than spending hours hunched over information technology indoors. They must have been much tougher and healthier than our molly-coddled Snowflake youngsters.

Reading 'Stalky and Co' was like a breath of fresh but savage air, fresh, that is, except for the dead cat under the floorboards.

547 words

3. IF AT FIRST YOU DONT SUCCEED -

My first attempt to read a Discworld novel by Terry Pratchett failed after a couple of pages. What weird science fiction, I thought. Wrong, wrong, wrong!

Fortunately the librarian found me three Pratchett novels when I asked for something a little different. They were certainly different, but no more Science Fiction than 'Alice in Wonderland.' A charming distortion of life on this planet, Discworld is modelled on a medieval drawing showing the Earth as a flat pancake, balanced on the back of a gigantic turtle swimming across the Milky Way.

The main characters are clearly human, but they are sharing their world with creatures we have met only in dreams, fairy tales and horror movies. There are zombies, so far doing nothing much; scowling dwarves working alongside humans, and big strong golems, willing but brainless slaves. Trolls, looking like huge rocks, occasionally get up and walk. So does at least one large suitcase.

Very occasionally we encounter magic. The College of Magicians keeps it chained down in books in their library vaults, crackling harmlessly. Books, you see, are very powerful magic. Death lives down there too, with his pretty young carer. He's such a charmer I would be honoured if he personally came for me someday – he usually sends an assistant.

The scenery of Discworld resembles that of Earth a few centuries ago. Towns are small, ramshackle and picturesque, and there are mountains, forests and plains. Their technology is what could have been invented but wasn't, or was but never caught on – very entertaining.

The leading human characters are, like the author's style of writing, quirky, intriguing and fun. There's Moist von Lipwig, a clever confidence trickster. He's trodden on the toes of the Dictator, Lord Vetinari, who gives him two alternatives: either be executed, or take on the running of the state bank and the post office, and construct a country-wide railway network, all at the same time, and for a low salary.

'Your life is the major part of your salary,' he says. 'A fair deal, don't you think?'

Moist's new wife, Adora Belle Dearheart, is a big tough horsey woman who runs the state telegraph service. She's very nice, really.

Discworld stories are not the only ones written by Terry Pratchett. One of his funniest novels is 'Truckers', a one off about gnomes, little four inch high gnomes, about the size of a coffee mug. Thousands of them live a well ordered life under the floorboards of an old department store. They watch, perturbed, as visitors stop coming and the goods, and then the shop-fittings are moved out. They discover that the shop is about to be demolished. They must leave or die.

'Prepare to meet thy doom, repent, repent,' say their priests. 'There is no other place but this.'

'But all the customers, all the goods, must come and go from somewhere,' say a few non-conformists. 'We must find out where that somewhere is.'

They find their way down to the loading bay, stow away on a delivery van and learn all they can about the outside world. Then they persuade their fellows to follow their lead, and pull each other up into a huge furniture van. Their engineers devise a series of ropes and pulleys to steer and change gear - and off they go.

The final chapter, as the huge truck bursts out of the delivery bay in the middle of the town and heads for the countryside is the funniest thing I've ever read. I laughed so much I had trouble holding the book steady enough to read it.

Finally, somewhat worse for wear, the truck blunders onto the no-man's land beside the airport runways. There it crashes into a small quarry and the gnomes set to work building themselves new homes.

'Those big flying things look interesting,' says one of the adventurers. 'They keep going somewhere and coming back again. We could borrow one and go see if there's a better place to live. They must be much easier to drive than trucks. There's nothing up in the sky to bump into, is there?'

'We could give it a try,' said another. 'Anybody game?'

683 words

PLAYS AND MUSICALS

PLAYS AND MUSICALS

You can learn a lot about writing plays by dramatising stories such as those of Charles Dickens. Try 'A Christmas Carol'. Just pick out the dialogue and leave the narrative behind, then study your text. Does it make sense? Can you follow the story? Does it need any stage directions to guide the producer or the actors? Don't spoon feed them. Leave them room to exercise their own imagination or to consult the novel. 'Enter Marley's Ghost, rattling chains' is the sort of addition you might need. Keep it down to a minimum. 'Scene four, a graveyard, enter Scrooge.' 'Scene three: Fezziwig's parlour, enter apprentices.' Trust the dialogue to tell the story. If tempted to turn narrative into extra dialogue first ask yourself if it really is essential to the story.

Dickens' dialogue is so good it needs scarcely any help from the narrative. He could surely have been a great playwright, given the opportunity. As a successful journalist, he was able to persuade his colleagues to print his novels a chapter a week as serials in their newspaper, a quick way to become a famous novelist. Shakespeare managed to join a troupe of actors, prepared to use the plays he wrote for them. Who you know has always been vital. A professional production of a musical can cost up to five million to stage. Impresarios would hesitate to risk so much money on an unknown writer without connections in the theatre.

To see your work performed you are likely to have to put in a great deal of work to get to know the right people. There are courses advertised on Google, taught by dramatists and directors.

The Royal Court Theatre appears very receptive to new dramatists, reading 2,500 new scripts a year and running short courses in aspects of the work.

You could join an amateur music or drama society with a record of putting on new drama written by local people. Many groups prefer to act their favourite shows, and know the audience is more likely to turn up for Les Miz or an Ayckbourn farce than for something they have never heard of. They need the ticket money to pay their costs.

If you belong to a lively community you might find the members ready to put on a play. Our community has recently staged Shakespeare, Dickens and Jane Austen in our restaurant – as dinner theatre.

Working as a professional actor or dramatist in the theatre is a very precarious way of making a living. Much less precarious is teaching English and / or Drama in a secondary school or college where you should find excellent facilities to stage your work, as long as it can be seen as educational. It is quite common to find the gymnasium sited behind the stage, doubling as a space for putting on costumes and make-up and for waiting to go on stage. Usually the stage is large and well equipped with theatrical lighting and the hall will hold many hundreds of people. Colleagues usually rally round to make the scenery, props and costumes and hundreds of unpaid actors and singers are begging for parts. I managed to squeeze 120 teenagers into a quartet of medieval mystery plays once. Great fun. Imagine the cost of a professional staging! It cost us almost nothing, and we made a good profit for the school funds.

So, before you write your play it is worth while thinking about how you could stage it. The more ambitious it is the more difficult that could be. It is unlikely you will succeed in the professional theatre without putting a lot of effort into trying to meet the right people in the right places. Obviously a drama course at a university or college would be a very good start. Good luck!

RADIO PLAYS

Radio plays are probably the easiest type of drama to cut our teeth on, and the easiest to perform. You could invite a few friends to dinner and a play reading. It would make a change from gossip and take little effort to organise. My radio play has only two main characters and two minor ones who could also do the sound effects.

TASK: Pick yourself a plot with lots of easy sound effects to bring it to life. It could be fun working out how to make the sounds.

ARREST ME, PLEASE!

GUARD: Mind the doors, please. (doors slam, guard's whistle, hiss of steam. Train moving off, clacketty clack.)

MURIEL: Goodness, what a rush! They'd hardly time to get their luggage off.

GERALD: Well, we're still running half an hour late. The driver's obviously trying to make up for lost time.

MURIEL: That was Blueberry Down, so Midwinter Ponds is next. We'd better be ready to get off pretty quickly.

GERALD: Mmm, yes. Move out of the way and I'll get the luggage down. (Sounds of train slowing down fast) We're here already. I'll jump out and you can slide the cases to me. (Shrieks of brakes, hiss of steam, door opening and cases sliding.)

MURIEL: Good grief! It's moving off already. I haven't shut the door.

GERALD: I'll shut it. (Sounds of running feet and door slamming.) That could have caused a nasty accident. Is the stupid driver drunk? (Sounds of train speeding up, then dying away into the distance.) Now the light's gone out. Can't see a blessed thing.

MURIEL: I don't think there was a light on. I think the train lights were lighting up the platform. Stand still till your eyes get used to the dark. Oh Goodness, look at that!

GERALD: What? What is it?

MURIEL: Look up. The Milky Way. Fantastic, isn't it, like a colossal firework display. I've never seen the real thing before.

GERALD: That just goes to show how dark it is around here. The power must be down for miles around. I gather this happens a lot in these little villages out in the middle of nowhere. I think I can see the ticket office. It's amazing what you can see just by starlight, isn't it. Pity the moon isn't out. Awooo! Blast it!

MURIEL: Gerald! What's happening?

GERALD: Just fell over the blasted suitcases, that's all. Better get them over to the ticket office out of the way.

MURIEL: Hello? Hello? Stationmaster? Is there anybody here? Hello? Hello?

GERALD: They should have emergency lighting. There's not even an exit sign. I thought there had to be an exit sign by law. Let's see if there's any light out in the street. (Rattles door) This door's locked. Can you make out another?

MURIEL: No, I don't think so. Seems to be the only door. Why on earth have they locked us in?

GERALD: Maybe our train was the last one tonight. It was so late maybe they thought it had been and gone. It's very quiet. Can't hear a thing.

MURIEL: (Owl hoots) Oh, Gerald! Where are you?

GERALD: It's only an owl, silly. We don't want to be here all night. Maybe we should try to force a window or something.

MURIEL: What if the village is on the other side of the tracks? Should we try to find out before we try damaging the windows?

GERALD: Good idea. I think I saw a bridge over the tracks. I'll go see if I can find it. Yes, gottit. (sounds of footsteps up a creaky bridge.)

MURIEL: Aooo! (Sounds of splintering and crashing to the ground.)

GERALD: Muriel, are you alright?

MURIEL: This step's collapsed. Could have broken my neck. This place has gone to wrack and ruin.

GERALD: Go back down. Don't come up. There's nothing to see, just countryside. The nearest lights look a very long way away. I can just make out a big long roof on your side. Let's go try to clean a window in the ticket office, see if we can see anything.

MURIEL: It feels filthy I'll never get that hanky clean.

GERALD: What a sense of priorities! Look, looks like a factory. Can you read its name? Is that an F?

MURIEL: Think so. F O R D something

GERALD: Ford's Factory Mid something.

MURIEL: Fords Factory Midsummer.

GERALD: Good grief! This is Midsummer Fords, not Midwinter Ponds. We got off at the wrong stop.

MURIEL: This station must be for the factory workers. They'll all have gone home by now.

GERALD: I think they went home a long time ago. Can you see all those broken windows? I think this whole place is derelict.

MURIEL: Listen! Is that a train? Flag it down, quick. (Sounds of pounding feet and train rushing through the station, then hooting.)

GERALD: Well, trains don't expect to be flagged down like taxis, I suppose. Hey, what's going on?

MURIEL: Rats! Oh, Gerald! Great big horrible rats. Help, Gerald, help! Get away you horrid beast! (Sounds of barks, snarls, growls and scuttling paws.)

GERALD: Get in the ticket office quick while I hold it off. Shoo, you nasty dog! Get away. Go chase your rats.

MURIEL: Come in quick and shut the door. Keep the nasty brute out. Oh, Gerald, what are we going to do? I'm sure the trains wont stop.

GERALD: I'll have to try to break a window. Trouble is, it's all tiny panes and lots of woodwork. I need something heavy to throw at it.

MURIEL: I can't see the point of getting out. There wont be a bus stop or a taxi rank, will there? Probably not even a working phone box. We'll have to stay here till day-light. Then at least we can see what we're doing. I think I saw a bench over by that wall. Let's sit down and think this through.

GERALD: Listen, is that a car? Look, car headlights. Thank Goodness! Try to attract its attention. (Sounds of car stopping, doors slamming.)

POLICE: Police! Police! Freeze .We're armed and we're coming in. Put your arms up and stand still.

MURIEL: Help! Help! Don't shoot us. We're innocent. (Sound of key scraping in the lock. Tramp of heavy feet.)

POLICE: Now we've got you. Caught in the act.

GERALD: What act? What are you talking about?

POLICE: Trespassing and vandalising public property.

MURIEL: We haven't touched a thing. We just got off at the wrong stop.

POLICE: That's nonsense. The trains haven't stopped here since the factory closed five years ago. I will have to ask you to accompany me to the police station.

MURIEL: Oh, yes, please. The sooner the better.

GERALD: How did you know we were here?

POLICE: An engine driver saw you vandalising the station and gave us a call.

GERALD: That's nonsense

MURIEL: Sh, Gerald. Where is your police station?

POLICE: Midwinter Ponds.

MURIEL: Perfect. Let's go.

GERALD: What I want to know is why on earth the train stopped and let us off here.

POLICE: Well, a driver did say he'd had to stop because there was a dog on the line.

GERALD: Well, there you are. Case solved.

POLICE: Well, then, we needn't detain you. I'll bid you goodnight.

MURIEL: Come on, Gerald, let's get in the car quickly. Officer, I insist on being arrested. Please bring those suitcases. They'll be vital evidence, wont they?

POLICE: Well, erm -

MURIEL: Come along, Officer. Let's go! (Doors slam, sound of car moving off.)

    1161 words

WORKSHOP TASKS

Use each of these sentences as the first or last line of your piece. See what you can write in fifteen minutes.

1. Sorry I'm late.   It was all because -

2. I couldn't place her - -

3. Agnes Weldon thought she knew him

4. It proved to be a bargain after all

5 It's good to be friendly, isn't it?

6.   You promised to be home by 6.30

7. Thank you notes

:Sorry I'm late. It was all because of - -

   - Machiavelli. My neighbour introduced the topic of Machiavelli when he blocked my way as I ran out to my car. He wanted to show me something on his smartphone, so I had to wait while he went in to get it, then scrolled through loads of pictures to find the right one. Somehow he mentioned Malevich, and then one thing led to another. Finally, up came Machiavelli, Cesare Borgia, Teresa May et al. We strayed onto Rome in all its glory – how could it crash out of power the way it did, then Egypt too. Along the way we brushed against Walter Gropius at the Bauhouse, Kandinsky being Machiavellian about Malevich, then Chagall got a mention too. Oh, and Father Christmas – how, as I'd predicted in my book, he'd chickened out this year for fear of being charged with inappropriate conduct with lots of little kiddies. Had I read Robert Harris on Rome? Was 'I, Claudius' one of his, or 'Quo Vadis?' Who could resist such a conversation?

* * * *

I couldn't place her at first, but then I remembered

   She had made strenuous attempts to disguise her appearance: her golden hair was now a dingy mouse and her eyes no longer looked so blue and sparkling.
   She pretended not to know me, but that sudden start when she met my eyes gave her away. She quickly set her face into a vague, unseeing look and turned to watch the bus slowing down for the bus stop. She joined the queue and drew out a smart phone, clamping it to her ear. I wasn't fooled. She was just trying to blank me out, to pretend I didn't know her, or even that I didn't exist. She must be cursing my very existence, wishing I would just evaporate and leave her be.

Of course I followed her onto the bus and sat near the entrance. She was using the black shiny face of the phone as a mirror, checking my every movement.

* * * * *

Agnes Weldon thought she knew him but she couldn't for the life in her place him - - -

Was it the milkman in his Sunday best, maybe with a good shave with a sharper razor? Should she smile as she drew nearer? If it was the milkman he would think her a snob if she didn't, but what if he was a total stranger? Maybe she should duck out of the situation into a shop or a cafe. She looked around the street. The shops and cafes were all behind her now. There was only a wall ahead, a high wall unbroken for maybe fifty yards. She would meet him right up close before the wall ended. Cross the street? There was a barrier along the middle and traffic thundered past.

He was much closer now, ginning inanely at her. And then she remembered. The dustman. Of course! The nice kind dustman who had helped her carry the old dog kennel out to his van. Oh, what a relief!

* * * * *

MINI STORY: It Proved To Be a Bargain After All.

RAPUNZEL

'Closing Down Sale, everything must go' said the notice on the window. What a mess! Nothing but tat. Why not sweep the whole lot onto the floor, shovel it into a wheelbarrow and out to recycling with the lot of it?

'Marm, can I have this dolly? Marm, please.'

'That one? Never! Find something a little more tasteful. Those colours are awful. '

'Marm, I love that dolly. I want that dolly, Marm!

I looked at the price ticket: £12.99 'It's too much money for a bit of reject rubbish and these colours are nauseating, all shocking pink net and puke green satin. Find something better.'

'No! No! I want this dolly. I love this dolly. I'm calling her Rapunzel.'

'You can't call it Rapunzel? It's got short fuzzy hair.'

'It's Rapunzel. I want it, I love it! I want it, I want it!'

Her shrieks were disturbing the whole shop.

'I could let you have it for £5,' said the manager.

Grimly I paid up. She had beaten me again. Why couldn't I discipline the little monster?

As I tried to buy a saucepan in the department store she dragged me over to the toys.

'Look, Marm, look! Rapunzel's sister. We've got to buy her sister!'

I caught sight of the price label: £19.99. What!

'Marm! Marm! Rapunzel wants her sister.'

'Rapunzel wants some tea and cake,' I said grimly – 'and yes, you can have an ice-cream.'

Well, Rapunzel. I thought, as I drank my tea, you may be in the worst possible taste, but you've proved to be a bargain after all. 269 words

FIRST LINE: **It's good to be friendly, isn't it?**

Spread a little bonhomie around this sullen world.

'That's a fine dog you've got there. What breed is it?'

'What do you mean, what bread is it? It's a dog. Or it was last time I looked at it.'

'Breed. I said "breed", not "bread".'

'How do I know what breed it is? All spare parts, init?' she snarled. Her teeth were even browner than mine.

The dog fixed me with its deep brown eyes. A low rumble began in its chest and erupted from its mouth as a snarl.

I backed off hurriedly.

'Don't show fear to a dog. It'll ave ya guts fa garters.'

Was that a twisted grin or a murderous scowl? On a face like that it was hard to tell the difference.

'Well, must be going,' I said hurriedly. 'So long.'

'Grr!' said the dog. 'Wuff wuff!'

Would you believe it? The woman let go of the lead.

Thank Heavens I can run! And I ran; you bet I did – but not fast enough. I felt its teeth brush my rump. It was either my big laptop or my backside. I swung around and belted the beast. You should have heard it howl! The woman, would you believe, was laughing her idiotic head off!

FIRST LINE: **'You promised to be home by 6.30,'**

she said. 'What time do you call this?'

'I did my best - -' he started.

'That's what you always say. I don't matter, do I? There's always someone else to deal with, isn't there? Every night it's just the same: working late. Is it that new secretary of yours?'

'Mary, it's your birthday. Don't spoil it,' he wheedled.

'Yes, it's my birthday, and you can't be bothered to get home to help me celebrate.'

'It's only seven o'clock, and the traffic was terrible.'

'It's the same for Frank next door. He was home by 5.30.

'So you check everybody in, do you?'

'I was looking out for you.'

'So, you saw what I've parked in the drive, did you? What do you think of it?'

'What's happened to your Jag? Is that a hire car?'

'You asked for a little run-about you could park easily.

"You haven't gone and swopped the Jag for that pathetic little heap, have you? What will the neighbours think? They'll think you've got the sack.'

'I left the Jag at the garage. They're going to bring it round later this evening.'

'Well, what's going on? What's it all about?'

'It's your birthday present, Mary,' he said quietly.

That's it, he thought. Why bother trying to please her? She wouldn't improve. She'd just get older and grumpier. Every birthday she'd be worse, older and older and grumpier and grumpier.

THANK YOU LETTERS

TASK: You know that Jennifer has sent you a very special birthday present but you can't work out which one it is. Write an all-purpose note of thanks.

Darling Jennifer,

What a lovely surprise! How did you match my taste so spiffingly? It's absolutely perfect. I'm showing it to all the family and they are all amazed that you have chosen a gift so fitting, so clever, so delightful. All my friends think the same. What a clever lady you are, Jennifer. Thank you again, with all my heart.

Your appreciative friend,

                        Joanne.

Next morning, the gift arrives late. Write the note that comes with it.

Dear Joanne,

I nearly forgot your birthday but thank goodness I didn't! I was passing the zoo when I remembered, and I had a brainwave. I remembered you spending ages watching the animals and saying how cute they were. Would you believe it, they had these baby rats needing a new home. They'll be very easy to look after. No need to feed them anything special, just let them out of the cage and they'll eat anything they can get their teeth into, slippers, cushions, curtains – just joking! Cat or dog food or just table scraps will do. They don't have names yet so you can christen them.

Love,

        Jennifer.

BOAT STORIES

TASK: Write a story about a small boat

IDIOTS AFLOAT

It was no day to put to sea, but we had only a few days of our holiday left - then it would be back to London and the grindstone.

We pushed Esmiralda into the still, grey water and clambered aboard. With no wind to harry us we had the tiny red sails up in a jiffy. We loaded our Mars Bars and cans of beer into the bucket under the thwart, then Mike grabbed an oar and pushed off against the river bank.

'There's sure to be some wind off shore. We've never met a flat calm out at sea, have we?'

He rowed us out of the Hamble into Southampton Water, then paused to assess the situation. The sails hung listlessly, the boom swinging this way and that as the waves set the tiny boat rocking.

'We could motor over to Cowes for lunch,' I suggested. 'Then have a walk around the town. There's a lot of it we haven't explored yet.'

Mike released the shock chords strapping the engine to the tiny foredeck. 'Engine' probably gives the wrong impression. This was no ship's propulsion unit – it was more like the motor of a small lawnmower. He lifted it easily and threaded it onto its brackets on the stern. One tug on the starter rope and it burst into life. Its maximum speed was four and a half knots. It chuckled away happily for more than an hour, then spluttered and stopped.

Mike lifted it up and gave it a gentle shake. It was unusually light. 'Out of fuel,' he said. He dragged out the fuel can from under the seat and handed me the big yellow funnel. 'You hold the funnel and I'll pour it in.'

Sounds easy, doesn't it. You try pouring petrol into a funnel on a boat that can't stay still for two seconds. No, the wind hadn't woken up, but the waves never sleep in the Solent. Even without the wind to blow them into furrows, the waves are stirred by ships of every size, from our tiny eleven foot Esmiralda to warships and even gigantic aircraft carriers. Half the world's merchant shipping thunders along the Solent, while pleasure boats of every conceivable size and shape skitter about amongst them. My sister calls it Boat Soup. She says if we fall overboard we'll surely fall right into somebody else's boat. We'd have to fall upwards, though: all the other boats tower way above us.

'Are you allowed to potter about in the main sea lanes like that?' asked a critic. 'It must be like riding a donkey right across a busy motorway.'

'Dunno,' we said. 'Nobody's ever told us that it's wrong – daft, maybe, but not against the law – we think.' And we had certificates from Plymouth Sailing School, stating our competence to be in charge of a sailing boat in near shore waters. There were shores nearby in every direction, and it's rare to see a no entry sign at sea.

Most people don't copy our example, not in eleven foot dinghies, anyway. Most people buy them to go around in circles, literally, around a race track on a quiet bit of shallow water. They find it exciting to get around a few seconds faster than the others. Why? We're explorers, looking for trouble like the Starship Enterprise. We can't go up the Zambezi and be back at our desks on Monday morning, and, yes, we want the best of both worlds.

'Full up,' I said at last. 'Let's have a Mars Bar while we think where to tie up in the harbour.'

'Depends what's there,' said Mike. 'We'll hang off something interesting, if we can. Get a close look at it, inside and out.'

That's what sailors do. Every evening you'll see half a dozen cabin boats, each roped to the next one, hanging off each space on the jetty. The people on boat number six have to climb over the other five to get ashore, but nobody minds - unless it's the middle of the night. It does wake you up with a shock, though, to hear somebody clambering about a few inches above your head, especially if they're blind drunk and singing sea shanties. You think you're being raided by pirates.

'Finished your Mars Bar?' asked Mike. 'Let's go. He pulled the rope to start the engine.

'Splutter. Splutter,' said the engine helpfully.

'Oh, come on.' said Mike. 'You've got lots of fuel now.'

'Splut.'

'What's the matter with you?' Mike demanded.

'Last time we ran dry we had to wait till it was stone cold before it would start again. Don't you remember? We could have a beer while we wait.'

'Weep! Weep!

'Whatever's that?'

'The Hovercraft, look!'

There it was, heading straight for us, bound for its berth in Cowes.

'We've got to get out of it's way.' Mike pulled the cord again and again.

'Slup', said the engine.

'It's still hot. Could you row?'

'There's no time for rowing. It's nearly on top of us.'

'Look out, we're here!' I yelled at the huge boat. Thank Goodness we'd had the sense to leave our little red sails up as a marker. Our tiny wooden boat would have been completely hidden by the waves.

'It honked at us. It knows we're here. It wants us to get out of the way.'

'How?'

'Goodness knows.'

'Power has to give way to sail, doesn't it?'

'Try telling that to a ship a hundred times bigger,' moaned Mike.

'Waap! Waap!'

'What now?' I moaned.

It was the hydrofoil, bearing down on us fast.

'Woom! Woom!' roared the car ferry. 100 cars and five hundred passengers bearing down on us too.

'We've had it, Mike. It's been good knowing you. Thanks for everything.'

'Noli illegitimi carborundum,' gasped Mike, still joking in the face of death. He pulled me down into the bottom of the boat. Well, he had to try something.

The noise had to be heard to be believed. Roaring, pounding, thundering, throbbing, howling, whistling as we clutched each other, waiting to be smashed into blood, guts and matchwood.

'Sorry, Esmiralda,' I whispered. We owed her. She'd got us out of quite a few impossible situations already. We had a penchant for stunts so daft that rational people wouldn't entertain them.

Gradually the noise passed its peak and began to diminish. We gripped the thwart desperately as poor Esmiralda rocked violently, threatening to tip us out. Who could blame her?

At last we dared to look up. We could see the backs of all three vessels as they headed into Cowes, while we bounced like corks in their powerful wakes.

'Idiots afloat,' said Mike ruefully. 'Of all the daft places to run out of steam, Cowes Roads must be the daftest. Why do we always have to learn the hard way?'

1144 words

TASK: Write some more idiotic boat stories.

IDIOTS UP THE CREEK

'Wind, at last. Look!' Mike exulted as he pulled back the curtains of the B&B. 'The trees are really dancing.'

I joined him at the window. The trees were certainly dancing, even in that sheltered garden. What would it be like at sea? 'Surely it's too wild for sailing,' I protested.

'Just what we need,' Mike enthused, 'especially after yesterday.'

Down on the dinghy hard the wind was rocking the boats.

'Great!' said Mike. 'Just what we want.'

'Speak for yourself,' I muttered. I'm an abject coward. 'Let's go for a walk instead.'

'We came here to sail,' said Mike reproachfully, giving Esmiralda a shove towards the water.

Why do I always do what he wants, however crazy, I wondered. Because he's irresistible. I want all his dreams to come true.

We had to scramble in quickly, as Esmiralda set off like an eager puppy. She was out in the middle of the Hamble River before we could even get the sails up.

'How fast can she go?' I wondered.

'Don't imagine anybody's ever bothered to time her,' said Mike. 'She's no racer; more a floating bathtub.'

That's why we'd bought her. The first dinghy we'd bought was a big mistake. It was by far the most elegant of the boats prescribed by the Trent Sailing Club, who raced on that inland river. We chose it for its looks, a 'Fireball' we named Apollo. Best for racing in calm weather, it went like a rocket, but the oversized sails seemed designed to capsize it, if hassled by waves or anything livelier than a breeze. It did its best to drown us. After one too many near-death experiences out at sea we sat in the boat park in Plymouth, watching a tiny tub with red sails doggedly make its way out to sea, unperturbed by the roaring gale that had grounded the rest of us. Whatever that is, we said, it looks like the right boat for us. So we sold Apollo and bought a Mirror dinghy. The sublime to the ee gor blimey!

Out in Southampton Water the wind was in a frenzy. Even Esmiralda's tiny sails were pulling fit to burst.

'I don't want to die just yet.' I moaned, as we fought to stop her careering headlong into an oil tanker, then ricochetting off the car ferry. 'There's an inlet over there. There might be sheltered water in that river.'

'Ashlet Creek,' said Mike, looking at the map he'd stuck down on the thwart. 'Goes in behind Fawley Refinery. Looks navigable. Let's go look.'

It was calmer on the little river, sheltered by the bulk of the refinery. There were stakes to mark the edges of the deeper water, so we happily zig-zagged up to the concrete deck at the end of the little creek.

'Let's go ashore, see what's here,' I suggested.

We tied the painter to a convenient ring and climbed onto the concrete deck.

'Oh, nice,' purred Mike, stretching out in the sun on the warm deck and closing his eyes.

Sunbathing gives me the screaming abdabs so I went off to explore. There were a few ancient houses and a nice old pub. 'Tea?' I asked the man polishing glasses.

'Tea! Honestly?'

'Yes, please. Tea for two.'

'Tea? I ask you!' he muttered as he trogged off to the kitchen.

How long does it take to make a pot of tea? Takes me about three minutes. What were they doing in that kitchen?

There were no disposable cartons for drinks in those days. I half expected mugs in this lowly pub, but no: out he came at last with the whole caboodle, tea pot, hot water jug, the lot. I stumbled half way back to the landing stage and just managed to stop the whole lot sliding off the tray.

'Well done, that lady!' said Mike, as he swallowed the tea with relish. 'Pretty good for soft southerners, hey?'

When he lay down for another doze I took the tea tray back, and chatted to the landlord for a while. When I returned to the landing stage Mike was staring down at the water. 'Come look at this,' he demanded.

Esmiralda was hanging by her painter like a picture on a wall. The surface of the water was way down below.

It was hard to release the rope with the whole weight of a wooden boat pulling at it, but at last she splashed down onto the water. We scrambled down the iron ladder into the rocking boat. The water was visibly receding down the wall.

Mike seized an oar and pushed off against the wall. The water pulled at Esmiralda like a traction engine. It swung her against a stake and left her high and dry. Quickly Mike wielded his oar and got her back into the current. Again and again the current beached her, while Mike fought to get her back to deeper water. She could float in only four inches of water, but at last the river won. We watched helplessly as the water's edge shrank further and further away. Now what? We rehearsed what we'd heard about the weird Solent tides. The tide stays high for hours, then retreats just a little, then creeps up again for a few hours more. Then, suddenly, it bethinks itself and roars out like an express train. It's all too easy to be caught napping.

'We could wade ashore, have a meal in the pub,' I suggested. We could see the pub quite clearly.

Mike poked the mud with his oar. It was soft black sticky quicksand. Worse still, the oar was now covered with shiny black oil, spillage from Fawley Refinery. We had no choice but to wait for the water to return.

'Lucky the sun's going down. We wont fry here in the open.' I said, trying to be positive.

Mike went through his repertoire of jokes to keep me laughing and I made up story after story.

'Hello, you folks stuck on the mud!' It was a man on the pub balcony. A few more men soon joined him, now work was over for the day.

'Want a drink?' one yelled.

'Yes, please,' we shouted back.

'Come and get it!,' they yelled, laughing themselves stupid. We were more amusing than the pub TV. They kept up a hail of insults till it was too dark to see us.

It must have been nearly midnight when the water came lapping back; then at last we felt Esmiralda floating. Even the pub had put its lights out, so, with no moon, we were almost blind. We blundered about in the river, going aground again and again, having to wait till more water came to rescue us again. At last we could see moving lights. We had reached Southampton Water, black as a bin-bag in the moonless night. Goodbye for ever, Ashlet Creek.

What on earth is that? Two large blocks of flats, a football pitch apart, moving in unison. An oil tanker, most of its bulk invisible between the lighted cabins at each end. Another even bigger moving block of flats, all its windows lit. A ginormous liner, Queen Elizabeth 2, on her way home to Southampton. Hurriedly we dropped the sails and put the engine on. We were invisible anyway, but needed instant manoeuvrability and maximum visibility to avoid these half invisible cities on the move.

Crack! What was that? Something must have smashed the propeller. Inexplicably the engine speeded up, and so did Esmiralda. That blow from something must have done her good.

'Look! The boatyard,' said Mike. 'We must have hit the Hamble Spit.' All sailors know to avoid that underwater bank of pebbles washed down by the Hamble as it joins Southampton Water. The boatyard is a landmark at the junction. We ricochetted blindly between the banks of the Hamble, but the rising tide was sweeping us up in the right direction. Soon we spotted the Warsach pub, lit by street lamps.

I staggered out onto the sand and toppled back into the water. Mike waded in and dragged me out. We were soaking wet and covered in sticky black sand. There was a hose lying on the sand, pouring water. What luck! We staggered about like drunks, laughing like crazy, trying to wash the filthy black oil and sticky sand off each other and off poor old Esmiralda.

A window flew up in the darkened pub.

'Shut up or we'll call the cops, you lunatics!' yelled a voice.

We slunk into the B&B soaked to the skin and oozing black oil. Thank Heavens our landlady had already gone to bed!

1440 Words

IDIOTS ON THE MOVE

'It's not too windy, look,' said Mike as he pulled back the curtains. 'and it's forecast to stay the same all day. We'll have a nice civilised sail for a change.'

Our landlady gave us a copy of the tide tables. 'You could get into real trouble without these,' she cautioned. How right she was! It had taken us ages to scrub the filthy black oil off ourselves, then off the bath after last night's escapade. We were highly motivated to do something sensible, for a change.

'How about a nice trip to Cowes for lunch?' said Mike.

Oh, what a good idea!

It was an uneventful trip for the first hour or so. Esmiralda's little red sails pulled nicely and Southampton Water in the daylight was a doddle, full of thrilling boats heading to and from the world's most exciting places. Someday we'd sail right around the world and see those places for ourselves.

Now, past the Calshot power station with it's landmark chimney and we were out in the Solent. Cowes here we come. Right across the main shipping lanes we fluttered like a little red butterfly, wondering which famous sailing boats might be waiting for us in Cowes.

'Have you changed your mind about Cowes?' said Mike suddenly. 'Off to Yarmouth instead?'

'What do you mean?'

'Look around. You should have Cowes on the nose and the Calshot Tower behind you.'

He was right. Both landmarks were behind us, one either side of the view. We weren't going from one to the other, we were leaving both of them behind. It made no difference how I steered the boat: the two landmarks continued growing smaller. It was a nightmare, surely.

Mike studied the tide table, now taped to the thwart. 'Lucky she gave us this, or we'd think we really had gone mad. It's the tide. It's running strongly down towards the Needles. We're going to be swept right out into the English Channel.'

'What if we end up in France? We haven't got a passport with us. We'll be illegal immigrants.'

'We might get washed towards the Channel Islands. That might be interesting. The tidal range around there is thirty feet. It's no place for little Esmiralda.'

'And we've nothing to eat!' I wailed.

'The tide will turn eventually and wash us back. We could put the engine on.'

Of course! That would solve the problem. With both the engine running and the sails pulling we'd surely be back to Cowes in no time.

We weren't. Cowes was still receding.

'What about the Spinny? We could try it out. The wind's not too strong.'

'Brilliant idea,' said Mike. He got it out of its wrapper in the bucket.

Can you deploy a spinny? Then you really are a seasoned sailor. They are the very devil to control. With just one fastening onto the top of the mast, the spinny flies free as a flag, an enormous featherweight bulging sail, far bigger than the boat. You have to wrestle with the bottom edge to catch the wind in just the right way. Our new spinny was in a co-operative mood that day. Eventually Mike got the hang of it and caught the wind, then Esmiralda took off like a space rocket. We were leaving a wake like a speed boat. Whihee!

Spinnakers are so big they block the view. They can wrap themselves around the unwary like a shroud or knock you overboard if you get too close. When at last we had a quiet moment to look out past the monster, the view was bewildering. Wherever had we got to? A line of buildings dead ahead on the far horizon appeared to block the end of the Solent. How could that be?

The boat was still whizzing along like a speedboat, so we let her carry on straight for the buildings. After half an hour or so her prow crunched onto a pebble beach.

'Excuse me,' I said to the nearest couple in deckchairs. 'Where is this place?'

'Lee on Solent

'Lee on Solent!' we gasped. 'Wherever is that?'

'It's very nice here,' said the woman, looking affronted.

'Oh, yes, I can see that', I said hurriedly.

While I searched for lunch Mike solved the mystery. We had somehow zoomed up to the point where the Solent turns to sweep down the eastern side of the Isle of Wight, far away from Cowes and the famous sailing Meccas. Portsmouth was just around the corner.

'By sheer coincidence,' he explained, 'the moment when we managed to get the Spinny to work the tide turned, It's now running in this direction at five knots. That, plus the engine's four and a half knots, plus the Spinney pulling so beautifully, and our little sails as well. Esmiralda was covering ground like a speed boat.'

It was still our lucky day. When we were ready to sail for home the tide had reached its lazy stage, coming up gently a little, then dropping gently a little, then coming up again. It would be an hour or so before it threatened us with trouble. We said goodbye to the deck chairs and pointed Esmiralda west. 'Home, Sweetheart,' we said.

'What ever's that?' I asked, A long wooden structure loomed, far away on the left.

'Ryde Pier, I expect,' he said. 'It's said to be a whole mile long, with a train running on it. Why don't we follow it into Ryde and have a look at the place, as it's so near. The sands are famous, nearly a mile wide at low tide.'

We pulled the boat out of the water and I went off to

find something for tea. We come from Yorkshire. We run on tea. It was hard to find a cafe that would let me take the tea tray onto the sands.

'Too many people never bring them back,' they said.

'How shocking!' said I.

Where was Mike? You can easily lose a man on a beach, but a boat? The sea looked strangely far away. I looked back to the prom and spotted Esmiralda, with Mike fast asleep right beside her. I trudged through the sand and kicked him awake. 'Look! Look!'

Mike shook himself, leapt to his feet and began trying to drag poor Esmiralda towards the far away sea.

Two middle-aged ladies, laughing like drains, leapt on him and pushed him away.

'Grab the engine, lad, to take a bit of weight off, and we'll get the boat on the water for you.'

Where did they get those weight-lifter muscles? They seized Esmiralda, ran right down the beach and waded into the water, with Mike, still a bit dazed with sleep, staggering after them with the engine and me trying not to let anything skid off the tea tray.

'Get in, lad, quick and get the engine going, or you'll be high and dry again in minutes.'

How right they were! With Esmiralda bucking like a bronco in the surf, I tried to get the tea tray aboard as Mike fitted the engine onto its brackets, but I didn't get a chance.

'Good luck!' shouted the ladies. 'You, girl, get aboard quick before the water gets away again.'

Have you ever tried wading through the waves chasing a bucking boat while carrying a loaded tea tray? Well, don't. When I did manage to catch up with the boat and plonk the tray onto the deck she washed away out of reach without me. Can you climb out of the waves into a bucking boat? Not easy, I can tell you. By the time I succeeded the tea was running all over the tray.

Mike steered the boat to the end of the pier and tied it to one of the legs. We had our tea and cakes drifting like a pendulum under and out of the pier. There's an art in picking up the cup just before the boat hits the pier and slops the tea all over the saucer.

'We've had tea in some pretty odd places,' mused Mike, enjoying a lump of fruit cake. 'We should write a book: Around the world on eighty tea trays.'

'Hello, you people under the pier,' yelled a voice. It was three lads fishing from the end of the pier.

'That's a bit of luck,' said Mike 'It's a two mile walk along the train lines to the cafe and back.' He shouted to the lads, 'Would you like to earn five bob?'

'Tell us how,' shouted the lads.

'I'll give you half a crown to take this tea tray back to the cafe on your way home. The name is on the cups. Tell them I promised they would give you another half a crown when you hand them the tray.'

After a bit of thought, two of the lads climbed down to get the tray and the money. We nearly lost the milk jug, but one of them caught it as it fell.

I still feel guilty about that tea tray. Did the boys take it back? Did the owners resent paying half a crown for it? Or did it languish on the railway track until some workman spotted it.

'How the Devil did this get here?' he'd say.

1524 Words

TASK: Write a story about a special boat.

KELPIE THE BEAUTIFUL

There was no mistaking the Sea Witch, lying quietly at anchor in the river that flows gently past the tiny Devon hamlet of Newton Ferrars. Forty years ago Kelpie was already an ageing lady, incongruous amongst the scattering of prosaic newer boats. Her cantilevered stern, carrying a little mizzen mast, echoed the slender prow that arched up to a long bowsprit that reached towards the horizon. Even under bare poles she was an Edwardian beauty, a relic of an age of elegance that, in the 1960's, already seemed a universe away.

From high above the river we gazed down at her in excitement and trepidation. We had paid to be part of her crew for seven days.

'Don't get too close to that parrot,' Andrew, the First Mate, warned me.

'The ship's parrot?' I was charmed.

'No way!' laughed Andrew.

'Come 'ere,' said the parrot, nodding at me and eyeing my sandwich.

'Hey, you talk, you clever bird.'

'Come 'ere, come 'ere'.

Mesmerised, I edged towards it. It seemed securely chained to the railings around the garden of the pub.

Suddenly, screaming and flapping, it lunged towards my hand.

'I did warn you.'

I shook my fist at the parrot.

'Come 'ere,' it replied, preening itself.

So, no ship's parrot, then. It was not the only thing missing when we four paying crew clambered up aboard.

'This is your chance to experience the great age of sail.' Peter, the Skipper, eyed us solemnly. 'No modern comforts when this old lady first touched the water. We have one sea-water loo, pump it in, pump it out, one gas hob, and that's it.'

'Showers?' I queried.

Skipper and mate laughed grimly.

'Half a pint a day to clean you teeth. Wash in a pub when we go ashore.'

I thought they were joking!

'Team work's what it's all about. Brute force.'

I swallowed hard. Feebleness has always been my forte. This crew was going to be one light. Perhaps they'd let me take the helm. I should be so lucky! We toured the ship. There wasn't much to see. There were ropes aplenty, carefully laid in coils, but where were the winches? Even our tiny dinghy had pulleys and jam-cleats. All I could see were giant wooden T shaped cleats, on the thick wooden mast and here and there on the bleached wooden deck.

'Prepare to sail. All hands on deck.'

We four stood to attention.

'Up mainsail!' The Skipper pointed to the correct ropes and we grabbed and heaved and grabbed and heaved and heaved! The gaff mainsail had a thick wooden spar on top as well as the boom below, so we were heaving up a tree-trunk as well as acres of heavy canvas. Sweat and consternation reigned.

Breathless and trembling with exhaustion, we turned our attention to the gigantic jib. Fortunately this foresail had no heavy spar on top. We watched its point creak towards the masthead in jerks as we heaved in unison. While we heaved, Andrew, big as a bear, had dragged up the anchor and the engine was throbbing.

'No mod cons?' I asked.

'Can't risk sailing her in narrow places. She's a fragile old lady.'

We looked at each other and swallowed hard.

'Take the helm, Jay.'

I scrambled aft, rejoicing in my luck. Where was the wheel? Down in a well in front of the mizzen mast was an enormous tiller. Could a tiller really control a 57 foot yacht? It was my job to find out.

The course was not in doubt - follow the river out into the sea - but steering wasn't easy. The helm seemed slack and offered me no feedback. Kelpie's sleepy response was so slow that I watched the bowsprit yawing this way and that across the view as I tried to feel my way. Fortunately the skipper's attention was else-where, checking the rigging and the coiling of the ropes. Andrew had gone forward to help with the final tugging.

The channel was widening now, and waves rolled in to meet us.

Kelpie's huge canvas sails began to slap and mutter as she headed towards the freshening breeze.

'Helm, bear away a touch to port.'

'Aye, aye, sir!'

As the bowsprit slowly slid across the horizon the chatter of the sails began to die away as the wind spilled into them.

'Helm, cut the engine.'

I leaned forward to push in the throttle. As the engine died the tiller came smoothly to life, pulling away from me. Kelpie was awake at last. Delighted, I pulled on the tiller.

Kelpie drew in a breath so deep it seemed to lift her right out of the water. Then down she rolled, head-first, and up again in that glorious corkscrew motion of a big sailing ship at sea, Out of the shelter of the land the sails pulled hard and it became an effort to stop her swinging back head-to-wind. I was glad when Mike joined me at the helm. Together we heaved like galley slaves, feet braced against the far side of the well as the water gurgled and slapped along behind us.

My watch as helm was over by the next change of direction, which proved even more taxing than I feared.

'Jay, you release the jib sheet, slowly. Get it down to the last two turns on the cleat and hold it there till I order lea ho!'

The jib sheet, a rope thicker than my thumb, was stretched like piano wire by the wind pulling hard at the huge foresail. By the time I had got it down to the last two coils I was no longer in charge of the rope. Creaking and whining, the rope had begun to move on its own, dragging itself around the wooden cleat.

'Hang onto that jib sheet!' Peter yelled at me.

By now the rope was dragging itself through my hands, taking the skin off my palms along with it. I had to let go while I still had hands left!

With a crack like a rifle shot, the rope leapt out of my hands and snaked across the deck, threatening to decapitate the crew. I ignored the skipper's interesting language as I inspected my red- raw palms.

It took three grown men, sprawled on the deck in a desperate tug-of-war, to tame that jib and get it safely cleated down on the other side of the deck. All my fault? No. Even with Andrew letting the sheet off at the perfect time it still took three grown men. We tacked only when we absolutely had to: to avoid running aground - or ending up in France. Coming into port we forgot the age of sail and used the engine.

Forty years on the memories of those seven days are still fresh and vivid. Hauling up the top gaff sail one day when the wind was light, then lying on deck, watching the great sails sweep across the clouds as Kelpie sailed fully-rigged in all her glory. Hanging out over the stern, watching the wake boiling and splashing when the wind was lively. Crawling out and wrapping our bodies around the bowsprit to watch the water hurtling toward us a few feet below.

Rowing back from the pub one night through water glowing with phosphorescent plankton, oars scattering drops that sparkled as they fell. Peter, lying inside the narrow pointed hull, watching the ancient planks as a strong head sea thumped and crashed against them. And Kelpie, with the setting sun behind her translucent sails, like a beautiful white ghost from another era.

It wasn't hard to understand how Peter and Andrew, two otherwise sane young men, could have come to devote their lives to this miraculous contrivance of wood, rope and canvas, steeped in the history of the great Solent races of Edwardian days.

Since that week so long ago we have made a habit of scanning every sailing scene for a glimpse of Kelpie, but Edwardian gaff-rigged racing yawls have been very thin on the water. I doubt if we have seen more than three in forty years, and none of them was Kelpie. Did the sea finally smash through that fragile hull? Did her owners go down with their ship? I suppose we'll never know.

But Happy Birthday, Kelpie, born in 1903, and 110 years old this year. Whatever your fate, you sail on in our imagination, your sails translucent in the evening light.

1416 words

* * * * *

**TASK: Write a story beginning with:
Julie exclaimed, 'It could end up either –'**

FULL FATHOM FIVE

'Is this wise?' Julie exclaimed. 'It could end up either sink or swim.' She pointed to the bottom of the boat. 'I don't think that's rain water. It's coming in through a crack in the bottom. Look, it's bubbling!'

'Stop fussing, woman!' boomed Harold. 'All old wooden boats leak a bit. Everybody knows that. Scared of a little drop of water? Pathetic little coward, aren't you?' He grabbed an oar and pushed off hard against the bank, setting the boat moving towards the middle of the pond. Then he overbalanced into the bottom of the boat, setting it bucking and wallowing as he dragged his heavy body up onto a seat.

'I've got a wet backside. It is leaking. Plug the gap with something, and quick, find something to bail it out.'

She searched the boat dejectedly. There was nothing at all in the boat. 'There's nothing,' she murmured diffidently.

'That scarf, try that,' he bellowed.

The lovely new scarf her sister had given her. She pulled it off, twisted it into a knot and tried to push it down towards the bubbles in the muddy water

'Get out of the way, woman,' he yelled, giving her a push. He banged his heel down hard onto the source of the bubbles. There was a sickening splintering noise and the bubbles changed to a gushing noise. 'Bail it out, you stupid woman!' he shouted. 'Do something useful for a change.'

Julie fumbled around under the rising water, finding nothing that would be any good for scooping water.

'There's nothing I can do. We'll have to swim for it. It's not very far to the bank.'

'You, swim?' scoffed Harald. 'I thought you were scared of water. You've told me that often enough.'

'That's why you made me get into this rotten old boat, isn't it, so you could sneer and laugh at me for being scared. Humiliating me makes you feel big. You're just a great big bully, aren't you, Harold.'

'And you're a miserable little coward, frightened of your own shadow. Scoop the water out with your hands while I row back to shore. Get on with it, quick!'

He picked up an oar and pushed it into the rowlocks, then scrabbled around in the fast rising water for the other, which set the boat rocking. The oar was jigged out of the rowlocks into the water. She watched it float away, out of her reach.

'Grab that oar, idiot woman!' he yelled.

'Are you sure it's me that's the idiot?' murmured Julie. The boat began to wallow around in a lumpen circle as he tried to row with one oar. He obviously knew nothing at all about boats. Or much else, for that matter. Why on earth had she deluded herself about him. She'd been so lonely, since Brian died.

'What did you say?' Harold lunged towards her.

Five years with Harold had given her hair-trigger reactions that had saved her from many bruises. Harold was so lazy he often didn't bother to take a second swipe at her when the first blow missed. She flung herself backwards and rolled out of the boat into the murky cold water. It wasn't as much of a shock as she expected. She soon got control of her body, wiped the water out of her eyes and began to tread water well out of his reach.

'Oh, it's quite shallow, is it?' said Harold. 'We can wade ashore.

'No, it's a quarry, about thirty feet deep,' she said. 'We'll have to swim for it.'

'Rubbish! I can see you walking.'

'I'm just treading water, waiting for you,' she said calmly.

'Nonsense, you can't swim. You admit you're scared of water.'

'Yes, terrified. That's why my parents insisted I must learn. And I'm very buoyant, can float very well, look.' She turned onto her back and pushed off hard against the sinking boat, sending it further from the bank.

'I can't swim!' yelled Harold. 'You'll have to help me.'

'How can I? I tried to learn life-saving but I'm too small and weak to hold anyone else's head up out of the water. We'd both sink. Sorry I can't help. You'll have to do your own swimming. You'll be fine. You're so good at everything, aren't you?'

As he lunged at her she swam away hard on her back, watching the action. The ducks were watching too, laughing their beautiful little heads off at the daft antics of these silly humans who kept trying to invade their world. Yes, she knew the experts said those calls were alarm calls to alert other ducks, but they always laughed in the right places, didn't they?

Harold's head, still yelling awful threats at her for her inactivity, slowly sank into the water, as the boat went down like a ponderous lift. The water bubbled and churned for a while, then everything was still and quiet – even the ducks.

Time to get out of the water. The sides of the pool were steep, but there was a bush just over there, growing on a ledge sloping down into the water. She swam towards it lazily. There was no need to hurry now. Harold couldn't chase her now. No need to run away and hide. She could have peace at last without running away, all alone in her nice little house.

If only Harold would finish drowning. She could hear the gasps for breath, the growling and burbling coming right up through the thirty feet of water. It sounded so horribly close now, right by her ear. She turned her head and there he was, mouth open, teeth a horrid brown, hairy nostrils, nose all red and lumpy with too much alcohol. It was all only a nightmare. A nightmare. Just like the whole of her life these days.

She struggled carefully out of bed and tip-toed towards the door.

'Two sugars for me – and make it good and strong. None of you horrible dishwater stuff!' he growled.

1006 words

TASK: Write a story called I Had a Dream

I HAD A DREAM

It was one of those hot, impoverished islands, the kind we all used to visit on our annual package holiday - probably Crete, or somewhere like that. Hot sun every day, cheap booze and fags, fried seafood in a dark taverna, followed by a wakeful night punctuated by numerous trips to the loo.

Bored with the shabby little village, and with stewing under a beach umbrella, we explored the far corners of the ancient crumbling harbour. We were newly into sailing, proud possessors of certificates from Plymouth Sailing School, showing our competence to sail a boat at sea, just offshore. We'd booked a course on coastal navigation. Then the world would be our oyster. We turned up our yachty noses at the lumbering, ugly gin palaces. Who on earth wants a boat without sails? They're just floating caravans, houseboats that rarely leave the harbour. Their owners lounge about sipping cocktails, dressed up like the skippers of great battle ships. All pretension: no performance.

Now there's a real boat, over there, where the jetty is crumbling. Not a fibreglass bath-tub either: a traditional boat, made entirely of wood, stripped bare of any varnish by sun, wind and water; sails neatly furled, and washing hanging over the boom – a sure sign of a real sea-dog. The clothes looked as worn and shabby as the boat.

A man came up from below and emptied the contents of a battered tin teapot into the harbour. The sun had cooked his arms like an overdone chicken, and bleached the hairs blond. His eyes were just twinkling slits in the deep wrinkles of a face tanned the colour of old leather. That's what happens to old sea dogs. The sunlight hits you twice, once coming down and once bouncing back up off the glittering water. It's the same with skiing. We'll pay for that some day, with faces just like this, maybe.

'He must be English,' Mike murmured. 'Nobody else uses teapots. Hello!' he called. 'Are you English?'

It was a while before the man responded. His mind must have been far away. He cleared his throat. It must have been a while since he last spoke. 'You are English too, by the sound of it. Where are you from?'

'Yorkshire,' I said. 'Does that count as English?'

'Wrong side of the Pennines,' he grinned. 'I'm from Manchester. We could restart the Wars of the Roses.'

'I love your boat,' I said. 'It's such a lovely shape, this beautiful stem and stern, all cantilevered out over the water. It's just the way boats ought to look. She must look gorgeous with all the sails flying.'

'Well, she's kept me safe up on top of the water for the last five years. Shouldn't grumble.'

'Five years sailing round the Med. Paradise,' said Mike. 'Our boat's only eleven feet long, but we sail her out to sea off Plymouth That's where we learned to sail. We're learning navigation so we can go places.'

'Been right around the world – twice. Not bad for an old boat. Knows her way, I suppose.'

'What? Right around Cape Horn?'

'Round every cape you can think of.'

'Wow!' I gasped. 'I've read that book by Joshua Slocum. The waves were so big they washed his poor wife overboard. She called out, 'Goodbye, Love!' Then the next wave washed her back on board again. What a miracle! Did you get very big waves?'

'One time, yes, but it was a mill pond the second time. Had to put the engine on.'

'You've lived our dream,' said Mike. 'When we've saved up for a boat like yours, we'll sail the world.'

'Well, good luck,' he said. 'Sell you this one cheap.'

'You're joking!' said Mike. 'We could barely scrape enough together for this cheap package holiday. It will take us years and years to buy a boat like this.'

'You could have this one for next to nothing – but I wouldn't wish it on you. Not seaworthy, to tell the truth. Needs thousands spending on it to make it safe to put to sea again, and I'm skint.'

'So,' said Mike, 'What will you do now: go home?'

'Home? Huh! Chance would be a fine thing. When the wife left me we split the assets. She bought a sensible little flat and I did what I'd always dreamed of doing, bought this boat and sailed away around the world. Sounds romantic, doesn't it? Well, it isn't. After the first three months all the harbours look pretty much the same. Some places you sweat, can't sleep for the heat; other places you shiver till your teeth rattle. One thing's always the same – it's bloody uncomfortable.'

'Honestly?' asked Mike, ' As bad as that? Everybody dreams of sailing off into the sunset and leaving all their cares behind. Surely you saw wonderful things.'

'Leaving all your cares - ? Is the boat about to sink? Is this scruffy harbour full of villains. Will they throw you overboard and steal the boat in the middle of the night? Dare you eat this mouldy food, drink this murky water? You've nothing else and you're miles away from land. Are you running out of fuel? Can you afford to get the engine fixed? Real, life-threatening problems.

'Take it from one who knows, who's run the dream to the bitter end. Stick to the day job. Save boats for the holidays. Dreams should stay dreams.'

'So, what are you going to do now?' I asked.

'Search me,' he moaned. 'Goodness Knows!'

                                              941 words

TASK: Write about losing your job

OUT ON THE SCRAPHEAP

A whirlwind spun into my room, slammed the door and came to rest against it. My feet paddled my chair around automatically to bring into view a caricature of Hubert as outrage personified.

'The Bugger's trying to fire me!' The words came spluttering from his puce and sweating face. 'He's gone completely loopy! He must be completely out of his tiny mind if he thanks he can make it stick. I'm a Director of the Company. He can't give me the push like any snivelling clerk. Who does he think he is?'

'The Managing Director,' I heard myself articulating slowly.

Hubert's eyes widened in apparent incredulity. 'David, we're a Board of Directors. We're jointly responsible in law for the conduct of this bloody company. He can't just chuck me out, just because I've got the guts to stand up to the dictatorial bastard. Somebody's got to keep his feet down on the ground - show him he's not God.'

'Unfortunately he's just demonstrated the short-comings of that point of view.'

Hubert took a breath - then snapped his mouth shut grimly. His brows met and he fixed me with a killer scowl.

'I see,' he snarled. 'You're in on it too. Know which side your bread's buttered. And I always thought you were a cut above the rest.'

'Hardly in on it.' I was surprised how calm my voice was; anaesthesia by shock, I suppose. 'I'm out on April 10th - allowed to get the benefit of two tax years for the pay-off. Such unaccustomed consideration, don't you think?'

The colour drained from Hubert's face. 'Not you as well, David? That's just ridiculous! Who could he put in your place? You've such a wide spread of responsibilities. There's no one half ready to step into your shoes.' A look of sudden understanding calmed his face. 'He's offered you early retirement on health grounds? You've taken advice on the deal, haven't you? I wouldn't trust the so and so an inch.'

I shook my head. 'No deal. Nothing. Just out. One year's salary and get lost.'

'He can't do this!" Hubert's colour returned in a rush. 'He's finally flipped his lid. We've got to get onto Geneva. They'll never let him carry on like this.'

'What do you suppose he was doing in Geneva last week? He must have cleared it with them already. He's fly enough not to get himself wrong-footed,'

'Then we've got to talk to the rest of the Board, get them to vote it out and demand an investigation by Geneva.'

I heard myself laughing drily. 'He's squared them all already, Hubert. He's given them all a bite of our empires and upped their salaries all round. Edward's to get my computers and Stephen gets Distribution.'

'What about Human Resources?' asked Hubert hoarsely.

'Our god Willie is going to take that on himself.'

'Grief!' howled Hubert. 'God help the poor Buggers! He's got about as much sympathy for his fellow man as Attila the Hun.' He slumped into one of my mauve designer chairs, his arms hanging limply over the squelchy sides. 'Hell, David, what are we going to do?' His body seemed to shrink like a wizzening apple, leaving only the eyes alive, glittering with feverish consternation.

'Join the infamous three million. Sign on for our thirty quid a week.' I grinned mirthlessly, trying to make it all seem normal - no great sweat and all that.

'I can't do that!' Hubert howled like a dog on a freezing doorstep. 'With my outgoings it just isn't on. It's alright for you, David; you've got a working wife.'

'Yes, I always had an inkling it could come in handy to have a wife on the right side of my balance sheet. You'll land another job, Hubert, sooner or later, but me - who'd take on a fifty year old Parky?"

'He's an outright sod - sack a sick man! Why couldn't he have given you an early retirement on health grounds? It would have cost him nothing. But no, not Willie Genghis Khan. He probably got a real buzz from kicking a sick man in the balls. If there were any justice he'd be flattened by a bus next time he crossed the road. It's just not fair.'

'Who said life was fair?' I got up and began to pack my briefcase mechanically. The Board Meeting agenda was on top of the usual enormous pile of bumph. Then the shock broke through at last. A wave of sick disgust hit me squarely in the gut. I seized the case and sent its contents thumping into the bin. To Hell with Board Meetings! To hell with William! To hell with the whole avaricious, profligate, shark-toothed lot of them and their pill-pushing sham of a company!

801 words

NOTE

This story was written by my husband. Good, wasn't he? Can you tell its author was a man, not a woman

LOST LOVE

Where have you gone, my bright and shining love?
Where are those arms, once strong enough
To swing me like a child up off my feet?
Where is that sense of fun, quicksilver mind,
So ready with a wicked pun, a joke?

Where is that bounding energy, that appetite
For challenge, both at work and out at play,
That laughing, striding man
Who carried both our skis?

Together, you and I, inseparable,
We flung ourselves at life,
Tried many daring things, enjoyed the kicks,
The adrenalin rush of danger,
Sometimes surprised to live to tell the tale.

Then, suddenly, the illness struck.
Like Icarus, you fell, shot in full flight,
Crippled by some jealous god, perhaps.

For years I tried to keep you on your feet;
Half carried you, willing you not to lose
The will to walk, to slump back,
First into a chair, then into bed,
Where teams of nurses dosed,
Cleaned and fed you day and night,

He was not old, you see.
Sometimes he whispered,
'I'm still here, you know, here, deep inside.'
And that hurt most of all.

Now I'm alone, tortured by guilt
Because I could not give him back his life.

Life was so good.
We had so much to lose,
And now it's gone.
It's time to pay life's bill.
Money is not accepted here.
Aching tears the only currency.

* * * * *

LAUGHTER IS THE BEST MEDICINE.

The best way to deal with a mugger
Is head-but him, as you would in rugger.
Then jump on his toes,
Ram your fist up his nose -
That's, of course, if you're very much bigger.

* * * * *

NOVELS AND AUTOBIOGRAPHIES

WRITING NOVELS

I hope you have used this book to practise making your work more effective. Now, instead of writing one thousand word stories, you may want to create a whole novel of about three hundred pages. All the things you have been practising still apply: you need to jump straight into the action from page 1. At the end, pull the plug before the boring clearing-up, and hop between scenes without explanations.

One new thing you need to do is create a framework to hang the story onto. The most popular ones are: a journey; a long struggle to reach a goal; a coming of age saga; a romance or a who dun it. A full length novel needs at least half a dozen highlights, evenly spaced, with quieter chapters in between. Write a synopsis of your story, spaced out over about 30 chapters. A big drama usually occurs about three quarters of the way through, followed by a reappraisal of where you are heading, before the build-up to the finale. Without this planning you could either finish the story before page 100, or reach page 300 with most of the story still untold.

The median yearly income of a professional writer in Britain is £10,500, so don't abandon the day job in a hurry. There are authors who make millions, but they are a tiny minority. If you are not trying to make a living as a novelist you can write in any genre you like, regardless of what the experts praise or say is most likely to sell. There are billions of books in print, covering every type of story and setting imaginable, so be brave: you can be as wildly, crazily inventive or as quiet and cosy and normal as you like. There are sure to be other books even more 'way-out' than yours. Don't worry about what other people think of it, as long as nobody gets hurt. It's your hobby.

PREPARING YOUR NOVEL FOR THE PRINTERS

First we'll assume that you are taking this sufficiently seriously to have bought yourself a full-sized computer and installed an acceptable word processing program. Publishers and printing firms accept work written in **Microsoft Word,** (quite expensive), but not Wordpad, or **Apache Open Office, free** to download off the Internet.

If, like my friend who had created six handwritten thrillers, you feel that computers are not for you, we'll come back to you later.

Do you have a few **memory sticks** plugged into your computer? It is essential to get into the habit of putting copies of your work on memory sticks and updating them regularly; then, if a chunk of your work disappears, or the computer breaks down, you need not panic – you will always have copies of your work. You could use a stick to send work to the printers, and to any friend prepared to download a copy of your work and read it. Ask the friend to warn you if you have written anything libellous or offensive, or given away embarrassing secrets.

What do you have on your screen? Is it a full-sized A4 document? You will need to turn your work into book-sized pages for the printers. Best do that now, then you can edit as you write, get rid of ugly gaps between words, and 'widows and orphans' – a few lonely words on the last page of the chapter. Rewrite to pull them back onto the previous page. You can then keep a check on how many pages you have covered. You need at least 70,000 words to qualify as a novel, about 280 pages in the Arial size 10.5 typeface you see here. This book, in **Apache Open Office**, has about 73,600 words.

Practise the procedure on the next page on an expendable document first so you don't make a mess of your novel, or use a blank new document page.

SHAPE YOUR PAGES

This book is written in **Apache Open Office**, Arial typeface, size 10.5, big enough to be an easy read. (If you use **Microsoft Word** their website will give you instructions for using their system. Ask Google for 'how to create a booklet or book' in Microsoft Word.)

A standard paperback novel in the bookshops measures 13 by 19.6 cm, the size of this page.

With your novel on the screen: (after you've practised)

In **Open Office**: Click on **edit**, then click **select all.** That should high-light your whole book. If you haven't started a book, open a new document and reshape that.

Click on **format**, then on **page,** then fill in the form that appears on the screen. 13 wide, 19.6 high, margins: sides: 1.8, top: 1.6, bottom: 0.8 orientation: portrait. Then click **ok.**

Click on f**ormat** again, and **paragraph**, then fill in that form: Click: **indent automatic**; **spacing above paragraph**: 0.10; **line spacing:** single, then click **ok**.

Page numbers: click Insert, then **footer**, then **default**.

Click in the new space at the page bottom, then click **Insert**, click: **Fields**. Click : **Page number.**

The page number has now appeared on the bottom left. Centre it if you wish. The lines creating a border do not appear when your work is turned into print.

What if I get in a mess and can't make this work?

If you don't have a helpful friend try a roving computer expert who will come to your home and sort things out, teach you how to deal with whatever is troubling you. They charge about £40 an hour. Ask around, look in the local paper, ask Google for local helpers.

Most U3A branches have members offering computer lessons in their homes, often free. They may never have tried this procedure, though.

HANDWRITTEN NOVELS

No! No! No! Can't be doing with all that!

Well, then, if your work is **handwritten** you will need to consider a self-publishing company. Be careful! Some could cost you thousands. They will offer to market your book for you, but they find it very difficult to persuade bookshops to display books by unknown writers. Some of my friends have books advertised on Amazon, but have sold scarcely any. If you are not famous nobody has any reason to look for your work.

Your handwritten text will be the first hurdle to surmount. It is not easy to find a typist prepared for the slog of squinting at your handwriting and trying to puzzle out what you are trying to say. You could not expect a friend or relative to shoulder the burden, and even typing bureaux are not keen. They are used to business jargon, which is predictable, and fairly short manuscripts, not hundreds of imaginative pages.

'But I have typed mine on my old-fashioned typewriter!'

It's not easy to turn such a script into a useful form. Every page has to be photocopied into a special program, which has to translate it into computer language. The result is not a pretty sight. It leaves you wondering what on earth you actually wrote.

I have tried dictating my work to a computer, but the result was useless, despite hours spent correcting it.

Forward Poetry have a sister company called Spiderwize who self-publish novels. They tell me they can provide a typist for a handwritten novel for £2 a page. That means about £600 for a 300 page novel. Then you would have a thick pile of sheets to study and correct. It's a safe bet that you would find something you wanted to change on almost every page. Then the typist would have to do all the alterations and send you another 300 pages - at whatever cost.

Probably it would cost at least a thousand pounds to get it into a final, corrected form you felt happy with. Then you would have to pay for editing and printing.

If you had sent them your work by email or on a tiny memory stick, they could have loaded it straight into their computer to read and then printed it. You would be a thousand pounds better off, which would more than pay for a computer and years of lessons.

Spiderwize seems a nice company that offers to print novels for a reasonable price, only a few hundred pounds if your work doesn't need typing up or editing, and if you don't mind signing a contract giving them almost total control over your work. Maybe that isn't important to you. Maybe most publishing companies insist on similar contracts.

So, how do we avoid signing over control of our work and paying a typist over a thousand pounds? Be our own publisher. Start by learning to use a modern word processor in a computer. Ask around for a visiting expert. Maybe find him first, then ask him to shop for a computer with you.

CHOOSING A COMPUTER

Apple computers tend to be popular with computer enthusiasts. **Microsoft Windows** systems are the best sellers so roving computer experts and neighbours are more likely to be familiar with Microsoft.

Most home computers are **laptops**, They are designed to be easily moved around, and many people carry them almost everywhere they go, watching films and emailing friends on the train to work. Computers are heavy, so small ones have become very popular. Many people have changed to a book-sized **tablet** now. My book-sized laptop is good for reading but not for writing novels. It is infuriatingly fiddly and too small to show the whole page as well as the word processing controls. These small devices are all 'touch screen,' so when you touch the wrong part of the screen the story keeps disappearing - embarrassing in front of an audience.

If you spend much time away from home maybe a big laptop would be best, if you could take it with you. **Laptop** keyboards are fixed to their screens so they are less comfortable to use than **desktops**.

The computer I almost live in is my huge **'All in One' desktop,** the kind you see in offices and banks. The screen measures 50cm by 30cm and contains all the machinery. It can show a number of documents at once, so I can move text around and do research at the same time. It is big enough to show films to good effect. It stays put in a cosy corner. The printer and everything I need is beside it on the desk. The separate keyboard can be put anywhere convenient. I can safely rest my fingers on the big keys, then the right amount of pressure produces predictable results. It is the most convenient and comfortable machine I have ever had, and comfort is important if you are spending hours typing your stories.

Away from home I write on paper - much lighter to carry than a laptop - then type it later.

When you have made friends with your computer you will have all the knowledge in the world at your finger tips, all in glorious colour and sound.

Now we have our computer we need to install the right word processing app., either **Microsoft Word or Apache Open Office (free**), both accepted by printing firms. Then we can type (two fingers will do) our own novel or autobiography. We can edit it as we type. The word processor will flag up what it thinks are mistakes and offer alternatives, but sometimes the suggestions are obviously wrong, so a dictionary is still useful – or ask Google. Google appears to know absolutely everything!

Now, what is next on the agenda?

PRINTING COMPANIES

Start looking for the right kind of printing company. There are lots of printers in the High Streets but most of them have no machines for binding whole novels. You may have to telephone a few firms to find the right one. Mine is on an industrial estate.

When you are sure you don't want to make any more additions or alterations, turn the text into PDF, that is Portable Document Format. To do this you will need to have **Adobe Acrobat Reader DC** installed (free) on your computer. Using Open Office simply click on **File** then **export as PDF'.** Then the PDF text will appear in the documents list after your original text.

You cannot alter a PDF document, so, if you are determined to make alterations later, delete the whole PDF, alter the original text, then turn it into a PDF again. A PDF prevents anyone else from tampering with your work and can be fed straight into the printer's machines. If you have any problems creating the PDF your printers may do it for you.

I take my novels to the printers on tiny memory sticks or email them. It takes them about a week to have a proof copy ready for me to take home and check, then about another week to print the rest. Their minimum print run is ten copies, which cost around £100 in total. Fifty copies cost around £200.

The printers do not read the text. They don't make any alterations so if anything is wrong it's all my fault. They do not ask me to sign any contracts. They do not claim any rights over the work, or take responsibility for what I have written. They simply print what I give them to print and I'm delighted with their work. They keep a master copy of my work so I can order more copies easily.

LIFE STORIES

RESEARCHING YOUR FAMILY TREE

This means creating a brief record of your ancestors, your bloodline bearing your name.

TASK: What's in a name? (? Your surname)

WHAT'S IN A NAME?   LUMB

'He comes from Halifax,' declared my professor, when I told him I was marrying a man called Michael Lumb.

'No, he was born in Bradford and grew up in Leeds.'

'Dig deeper, and I'll bet you'll trace his ancestors back to Halifax. All the Lumbs come from Halifax.'

Remember Professor Higgins, who knew which street Eliza Doolittle was born in? Well, my professor could place anyone born in any Pennine village. People still retained their ancient dialects in the 1950's, with a strong Viking influence. Few people had TV and the voices we heard on films and radio sounded like upper class aliens. Anyone trying to ape them would have been ridiculed.

My brother-in-law researched the history of the Lumbs, hoping to find a few noteworthy ancestors he could be proud of. He searched the Public Records Office and parish registers for years. In fact, it seems that all the Lumbs in History, apart from Mike and his brother, were lowly labourers on the land or in the factory. One Lumb in the Thirteenth Century had been Lord of the Manor: not, however, an important or aristocratic title.

According to Google's data banks, the Lumb family has always been far from robust, hovering on the brink of extinction. The Census of 1900 registered only 3,000 of them in the whole country, most of them in Yorkshire. I appear to be the only Lumb in my town, and it's only my husband's name, not mine. We have no descendants so yet another branch has died out.

Lumb is a variant of Lamb, and signifies that the bearer of the name is a gentle, kindly soul, as both Mike and his brother were. Amazing that such personality traits could persist from before the Norman Conquest, for Lumb is an Anglo-Saxon name. That didn't surprise me. Mike had blue eyes and thick fair hair, like a German.

Lumb is also a variant of Lumm, Anglo-Saxon for a pond or stream, and a pond below a waterfall. Mike certainly loved water. He coaxed me into having a pool installed in our garden and swam every day in summer, always insisting I kept him company. Having seen a friend drown, I was terrified of water, but he managed to get me into a dinghy and we sailed out to sea singing sea shanties. Then he discovered that some very famous yachts were defraying their costs by accepting experienced paying crew for holidays. Half-way between Dartmouth and Alderney in the Channel Islands the mast of our Americas Cup winner cracked in half and toppled over the side. Getting back to Dartmouth took ten hours, through the coal black night with no lights to warn other shipping we were there.

Lombard seems a fine imposing name, the name of a wealthy banking family, but sadly it has no connection with the lowly Lumbs. Nor does Lamm in China, nor Lund or Lun in Scandinavia.

Lumb is a rare and delicate little name which could be an advantage. I first published my novels under my own name, Shaw, then found them included in a list of works by another Jay Shaw. Hands off my books! Shaw is a far more robust, aggressive name. There appear to be millions of us, so it's not easy to stand out in such a crowd. I have republished my work in my married name. There are so few poor little Lumbs about that my work should not be mistaken for anyone else's in future.

600 words

ILLUSTRATED AUTOBIOGRAPHIES

An autobiography is the story of your own life, not your family history, so thinking about it, dredging up memories is the type of research you need to do. .

Let's pause a moment and try to picture our friends and descendants owning the finished product. If your autobiography is a mess of bits and pieces and needs a container to keep it together, how often are your progeny likely to root it out of the back of the cupboard and litter the table with it?

Many of us have made cine films, videos and digital films on phones or computers. Sadly, our descendants may not be able to watch them. Projectors to show cine and video went obsolete years ago and our present day discs, phones and computers may soon do the same. Will anyone bother to convert our films to a future new technology? They will probably be thrown out with the old hardware. If you enjoy making films don't abandon a good hobby, but we need something more durable too.

Books, in one form and another, have survived for thousands of years. Downloads onto Kindle-type devices were forecast to obliterate books, but, instead, it seems to be the downloads that are now dwindling and the books are rising in popularity again. You can't wipe off a real book by accident and you don't need the latest technology to access it.

So, let's concentrate on putting your life-story in a book. If you want to include lots of photos it had better be a big book, A4 size. You can squeeze in ten times as many photos if you make them into collages. Cut the most interesting bits out and stick them on a backing sheet. Don't worry about lumpy over-laps – they will all be ironed out when you photocopy them. You can use a colourful collage as a cover as well. You can group the photos into themes or people, put numbers on important pictures and identify them on the facing page.

If you can't use a word processor for the text, I hope your handwriting is easy to read. The simplest method then must be to produce a dozen copies for family and friends by photocopying the pages and fixing them in covers from a stationers - an attractive present to sit neatly on a bookshelf amongst the tall books. Keep a copy that can be taken apart easily, in case you need to photocopy an extra one later.

If your handwriting is hard to read you could try to improve it. Loopy old-fashioned Copperplate done badly looks an ugly tangled mess. A modern style is easy to acquire. Write out: 'ago, dogo, goda, pango, bongo' until the round shapes all look the same size and basic shape. Write each tail as a single downward stroke, like the print in this book. Don't bother practising any other letters – that seems to make bad writing even worse. No prizes these days for joining all the letters together.

NARRATIVE AUTOBIOGRAPHIES

An autobiography could be more difficult to manage than a novel. It might be worth spending some time thinking about your future readers and trying to imagine what they might be looking for in giving up time to read your work. People who knew you might want to read about themselves. Future generations of your family might want to know who bequeathed them their red hair or fiery temper. History buffs might be fascinated to read about life-styles and attitudes of people in past ages.

You could waste a lot of time checking up on dates and names of places you have lived in or visited and the hundreds of people you have met, all of which may be of little interest to anyone else. A strictly chronological account could become a chore to write as well as dull to read. You may run out of steam and never finish it.

It might be more fun to write your autobiography as a series of short stories, each bringing to life some aspect of an era or a memorable part of your life. People like stories they can tell to other people. 'My great grandad was amazing. He did - - .' Writing separate episodes means you don't have to start with the day you were born: you can do that later. You can start work on whichever episode comes most vividly to mind, then easily arrange them in order later, or keep that episode as a baseline from which to reveal your life in a series of flashbacks.

TASK: Write the first chapter of your life

Compare the following pieces with each other and see what you can learn.

No.1: MY DAD

I was born in a slum, the first child of an unemployed labourer. It was early January, and Huddersfield, Yorkshire, was at its worst – snow fluttered down through the heavy pall of sooty smoke pouring from a forest of tall mill chimneys. Our tiny back-to-back house had no kitchen or bathroom, and no hot water, except for the kettle singing on the metal shelf attached to the firegrate. There was a single loo outside in the yard, shared with three other families, who took turns to cut newspaper into squares to hang on a string beside the pan. Jeremiahs under the beds and a tin bath in front of the fire on Friday evenings were the norm. We didn't feel deprived. Everyone we knew lived in similar conditions. I was nine, and the eldest of three daughters, when we moved to a house with a bathroom and kitchen.

I shudder to think what my life would have been if the 1944 Education Act had been passed two years later. My family was disconcerted when I passed the brand new Eleven Plus Exam and qualified for a place at grammar school.

'She'll grow up to be a dreadful snob,' everybody told my parents. Fortunately they believed they had no choice in the matter. The Authorities had decreed it.

'No way can we afford that silly uniform.'

Somehow pieces of uniform found their way to me, all very worn, but wearable. The overcoats always seemed to be some other school's colour. I was told off regularly about them but what could I do?

It was an alien world, this school full of polite, quietly-spoken, knowledgeable people. Workers learn to shout over the noise of the factory machinery. The lessons were easy to understand, and after the first year I was put in the top form, to study Latin for university.

The school leaving age had gone up from 14 to 15.

'You start work in the mill on Monday,' said my dad, who left school at 13. 'Time you earned some money.'

'But I have to sit my 'O' Levels next summer. If you make me leave school I'll leave home,' I challenged him.

'Go on, then. One less to feed,' he growled.

So, I caught the train to London, to stay with a former neighbour who had moved to Ealing. Every penny I earned in Woolworth's went to pay for my bed and breakfast. When I had lost a stone in weight and two teeth to malnutrition I got an evening job in a cinema as well to pay for lunch and supper.

After eight weeks my father rang to beg me to go home. His workmates had told him he would go to jail for claiming child allowance after I had left home. I expect he assumed I'd crawl home within a day or two.

'If I come home I'm going back to school,' I declared.

At sixteen, having passed nine 'O' levels, I told the headmaster my dad refused to allow me to stay on for 'A' Levels, so he visited my dad at work. He was a big, imposing man and must have scared the daylights out of Dad, who then contented himself with snide comments about idle bitches reading books while real people worked. Next school holiday, while working as a bus conductress, I contrived to work a hundred hours in one exhausting week. I put my pay slip in front of him and said, 'Now who's an idle bitch? Beat that!'

My father taught me a lot in addition to fighting my corner. He had been offered a place at Grammar School himself but his family had vetoed that. Though he'd left school at thirteen he was very well read, and loved an argument, no holds barred. I had to make sure I was nearer the door than he was if his temper boiled over when he was losing an argument. I learned to enjoy those evening walks as I waited for his fury to cool down.

Looking back I feel ashamed of upsetting my Dad. He was a very hard-working, clever man who deserved a prestigious job, but fate and his family had kept him in the gutter. He had no father, and his mother had been destitute and so hungry that he had been born under-sized and damaged by rickets. His grandparents, who reluctantly brought him up, deliberately humiliated him.

But if I had not defied him I would have missed out on a very rewarding life. My younger sisters also benefited from my trail-blazing. In the end he was pleased that I made the most of my chances. When his grand-parents died he blossomed and started to seek out the good things of life. Heart problems got him early retirement at sixty, but he lived to be 85, a very good age for a man of his generation. They were very happy years as well. He went to live at the sea-side, travelled the world and enjoyed his hobbies right to the end.

They say that being undernourished in your youth can give you a longer life. Maybe there's some truth in that.

828 words

No 2: I REMEMBER, I REMEMBER

The house where I was born was a Victorian slum, one of a long terrace of hovels built by the local mill-owner for his workers. In the 1880's a flood of near-destitute country people washed into the new towns as the Industrial Revolution gathered pace.

My parents moved in from a single room nearby, and were thrilled with their new home. It had a living room with a bedroom and a tiny box room above. A new water main had just brought water into the houses at last, one tap in the coal cellar for the washing and the other at the top of the cellar steps.

The tiny living room had a Yorkist range, a sort of ancient Aga, with an open fire alongside an oven heated by the hot smoke. The metal ledge at the front of the fire-grate was our cooking hob, The tin bath hanging above the cellar steps was brought down every Friday evening and filled with water warmed on the fire in a kettle and a saucepan, both caked with burned-on soot. We lined up to be bathed, first the baby and lastly Dad, covered in a week of factory dirt. Then the dirty water had to be scooped out and tipped into the sink at the top of the cellar steps.

The terrace was back-to-back: our back wall was shared with my aunt's house that faced the cobbled street. We had to walk through a little tunnel leading to the yards of the rear-facing houses. We faced a narrow unmade alley that had, until recently, been used by the night soil men to empty the tub of excrement from the outside loo. Now the new water main had given us a wonderful flushing loo, shared with three other families. We took it in turn to cut up newspapers into squares and hang them on a string beside the pan.

Most of the local adults worked five and a half long days a week in the mill, so when not in school the kids ran wild, shouted at by anyone at home; women with a pre-school brood and old ladies who somehow managed to subsist. Old men were rare: they usually worked till they dropped.

Though they had left school at thirteen, my parents were intelligent and had read about birth-control. They spaced us four years apart, so they could give each of us lots of attention. With me aged nine and the youngest only one, we actually had no interests in common. We had to fight for space in the single bed we three shared. It's amazing the baby survived.

We didn't know we were deprived. Everyone we knew lived in similar conditions, my aunt behind us, my grandparents next door and another aunt further down the street. To socialise we sat on our doorsteps and passed the news up and down the terrace.

My mother had a crazy sense of humour and was relentlessly cheerful, so it was a shock to see her crying one Thursday. She had lost her last shilling and could not buy the meat paste she had planned for my dad's sandwiches. He would have to shovel coal all day, fuelled by nothing but jam and bread.

By the time I was nine my dad had been promoted from throwing coal into the deep fire-grates inside the boilers. Now he was in charge of the engine, the huge fearsome beast that powered the hundreds of machines that spun and wove expensive woollen suiting. He could now afford more rent, so we moved into a house with a bathroom and a kitchen. It had only two bedrooms, but one had room for three beds.

We three girls still had reason to fight. At fourteen I saved up for weeks to buy my first lipstick. My six year old sister drew pictures on the bathroom mirror with it, then ground it into the fluff under the bed.

'Don't bully the poor little thing,' laughed my mother. 'She was just having fun.

'Bully her? I'm going to murder her!' I howled

'689words

No 3: HUMBLE BEGINNINGS

97 College Street, Crosland Moor, Huddersfield was not a pretty sight at the best of times. On January 7th it was spectacularly dreary. Frozen drizzle leaked from the khaki coloured fog. If only it would snow and cover up the dismal little yard where not even weeds would grow!

There was a fire in the bedroom grate. My mother shivered as my father opened the door to bring in a bucket of hot water from the cellar. It was his first experience of childbirth and he had no idea what to expect. Luckily the midwife arrived just in time to pull me out into the world at about six-thirty am. Apparently I screamed blue murder. I'm not surprised. I often wondered if I'd been a dreadful reprobate in a past life and this life was my punishment.

The terrace house with a living room and a cellar, half-full of coal, eventually housed five people, we three sisters crammed into a single bed in the tiny box room. We had no kitchen or bathroom, only two cold taps, one in the cellar for the washing and one at the top of the cellar steps. I was nine before I turned on a tap and found hot water coming out of it. In the tiny living room there was a Yorkist range, a sort of ancient Aga with the oven heated by the open fireplace. A metal step across the front of the fire-grate was our cooking hob, with space for a soot-blackened kettle and a saucepan.

Imagine giving birth in a place like that! My poor mother had to endure that twice. She was delighted when she was allowed to have her third child in hospital.

My parents didn't grumble. They were thankful for what they'd got, having grown up in even worse conditions, with a host of siblings and brutal parents. We had caring parents who planned our arrival with four year gaps so they could give each of us lots of attention. That was in the days when birth control was a very new idea. My dad worked hard – when he could find a job, and gave his pay-packet to my mother unopened every Friday evening. She thought carefully about every penny she spent. It was a spartan life, but they never got into debt. They paid a small sum every week into a fund they then claimed back for Christmas presents and a day at the sea-side. When a dire shortage of rental property forced them to buy a house, my dad was very unhappy about the 'mill-stone of debt' hanging around his neck.

How old are babies when they first learn to crawl upstairs? That was the age of my earliest memory. It must have been summer. I remember bumping down the stairs and hitting my head on the flat iron propping open the out door. Maybe that explains my dreadful memory, or my inability to get to grips with Maths and German. I expect my mother just put me back on my feet and laughed. 'Don't make a fuss.' According to her, every problem would 'sort itself out' if you ignored it. She steadfastly refused to take anything seriously and laughed and sang all day. When we told her our doings she would turn them into an impromptu opera. Of course we all joined in. We grew up uninhibited and noisy. Maybe we were the neighbours from Hell. Maybe they were glad to see us moving out. We were delighted.

The new house was a palace. It had a kitchen with a gas stove that didn't cover the pans with soot. There was a small room with a bath actually fixed to the floor. We could turn on the taps to fill it with hot water, then pull out the plug and see it empty itself by magic. And there was a loo, actually inside the house! No more braving the weather to rush down to the end of the yard. Gleefully Mum had left the chamber pots behind.

681 words

WRITING THE FINAL CHAPTERS

Well, now that we have a few ideas for Chapter One of our autobiography we should list the most exciting or moving things we have not yet put into our manuscript and write them as soon as possible.

How to end our story? Can we end it? An autobiography that ends in the middle of a sentence when you have gone off to do something interesting – or die - may sound intriguing for future readers and maybe leave them wishing for more. But more likely an unfinished work would be binned.

And we shouldn't leave it too late, or senility might scupper the whole project. A tatty bundle of paper might go straight into the recycling bin, along with a few memory sticks. We must call a halt in good time and get it into print inside a smart-looking cover.

Give it a chance to survive us.

TASK: 'The road not taken' - that might have led to fame and fortune.

THE ROAD NOT TAKEN

It must be in the DNA – the way adolescent girls are smitten by a crazed devotion to some famous figure, usually a pop star in our culture. It must be there to make them rush into the harem of some powerful alpha male, no coercion needed.

Everybody thought my crush bizarre. I was thirteen when I was taken to see the Laurence Olivier film of 'Hamlet'. Shakespeare? Wasn't he that old cove who wrote that daft play, 'A Midsummer Night's Dream'? Never mind. I could pass the time day-dreaming in the dark cinema.

I day-dreamed through most of my lessons at school - they were so slow and dull. When alive to my surroundings I livened up the dullness by disrupting the lessons. I often wonder why they didn't boot me out. Well, I was one of the first kids from the working classes to be offered a free place in a grammar school. Maybe I was just what they had been warned to expect. Bless them all! And I had this infuriating habit of waking up and doing pretty well in exams. Well, exams were quite exciting, weren't they – and so easy.

So, at thirteen, I saved up my pocket money and bought 'The Complete Works of William Shakespeare.' I read it from cover to cover, then read it again and again. I played games with it. In which play do they exeunt bearing out the most dead bodies? 'Titus Andronicus', of course. I could soon declaim most of the famous speeches by heart. When I grew up, I declared, I was going to be the new William Shakespeare for our time.

My long-suffering school gave me elocution lessons to tame my broad Yorkshire accent and entered me for acting exams, adjudicated by a teacher from the London Academy of Music and Dramatic Art. When she handed me my certificate marked 'Distinction' she gave me application forms and suggested I should apply for a place. She felt sure her college would accept me.

'Is that wise,' asked my teachers. 'Have you noticed that most plays have far more parts for men than for women? Actresses spend most of their time begging for someone to give them a part, any part. You need to earn a living. Why not get a university degree first as a fall back? Leeds University has a famous Drama Society. You could keep up your acting with them.'

Well, the school had given me star roles in two operettas and a few plays, so it was easy to persuade the Leeds society to do the same. Things looked very promising. Then the Suez war was declared. Funding for PhDs was withdrawn and my gorgeous fiancée was ordered to report for National Service. Oh horror! It seemed a good idea at the time to get married before he went off killing all those nice Egyptians, simply for nationalising their canal.

When I graduated a year later I viewed my assets. Yes, I could sing higher and lower than most people but my voice wasn't loud enough for the professional theatre. Microphones were cumbersome and ugly then, and not used in operas, operettas or musicals. My legs are too short for a chorus line and I'm far too prudish (chaste?) to 'sleep' my way to good parts. The plays I wanted to write, musicals and glamorous, cheerful, funny, upbeat stuff, had suddenly gone out of fashion. 'Look Back in Anger' had started a trend for grim, violent plays set in the working class that I was trying to crawl out of.

Besides, I had a starring role all ready to walk into: the wife of a handsome RAF officer with a delightful disposition. We'd been apart for more than a year, and had little chance to play husband and wife.

We were both skint, both from homes in the slums with no bank of Mum and Dad. I played bus conductress again (great fun) and clerk in a tax office (gave me the screaming abdabs, and so did a stint in a gift shop.) Finally my gorgeous husband rubbed my nose in an advert for an English teacher at the local college of Further Education.

'No! No!'

'Yes, yes. We need the money.'

Yes, teaching was every bit as bad as I'd expected. I was tempted every morning to get off the bus, cross the road and go back home, but I'm not a quitter. Working class people know they have to work. So I worked. I was lucky to get a few disruptive youths in my classes. I understood them, and came to enjoy sparing with them.

When Mike left the RAF and moved to Derby to work for Rolls Royce I reluctantly took a job teaching English and Drama in a secondary modern school. It was newly built, and had a superb Assembly Hall with a wrap-around stage and amazing stage lights. The Council sent a theatre technician to teach me how to use the huge control board. I could flood the stage with a rainbow. Wow! This called for something exciting.

It proved far too expensive and complicated to hire scripts and performance rights: it was much easier to write my own dramatisation of 'A Christmas Carol'. The following year I translated and dramatised four medieval plays and staged them with a cast of 120. Eat your heart out, Cecil B De Mille! Teaching was not so bad, after all.

Next, working in a grammar school, I directed a few plays, including Wilde's 'Importance of Being Ernest.' Later, as a Deputy, then as the Head, I trod the boards almost daily, in front of audiences of over 800. No half-empty houses for me: all command performances. My job became so demanding there was no time for plays, and no fiction could compare with the almost unbelievable reality - exciting as a roller-coaster ride.

So, I never did become the second Shakespeare, but who did? Nobody did, did they?

And I never had to beg scornful impresarios to finance my plays. I never had to plead or 'sleep' with ugly old producers to secure a role in a run of-the-mill play in a decrepit half-empty theatre with shabby airless dressing rooms. I never had to be on set at 5 am in the rain to shoot some dismal film or TV show. I've lived my own life story, with a co-star who couldn't have been more delightful. We explored the real world and did many very exciting things.

Fame was never a problem. Descartes said, 'cogito ergo sum – I am thinking, therefore I exist.' Today we have different proofs of existence: 'I have a media presence.' I've seen my own face illustrating half-page spreads in a number of respected national newspapers and appeared in BBC programmes. As the Head of a successful High School I was invited to address a party conference. This headline: 'Clone that Head', then appeared in the London Evening Standard. An MP had declared that 7000 clones of me could cure all the problems in Britain's 7000 High Schools. What a joke!. I could have used a few of those clones to share my workload!

So, I'm not the least bit sorry that my dreams did not come true. How could a world of shabby make-believe compete with a genuine life like this?

1210 words

TASK: Write the story of your life.

THE STORIES OF MY LIFE

Long before the invention of writing there were stories, stories that intrigued me from the age of six. In my teens, pleading rheumatism to avoid freezing cold games lessons, I persuaded the Headmaster to let me research ancient history in the school library instead. He no doubt planned to catch me out and sling me out, for I was notoriously troublesome. Some of my teachers dropped in to cross-question me about my research and retreated puzzled, to discover that I did indeed have an encyclopedic knowledge of the heroes of pre-history through cross-referencing them in the Encyclopedia Britannica. Of course it was a ruse to stay in the warm indoors, but I was genuinely enthralled by that whole universe of fascinating characters.

By the time these stories first appeared in writing about three thousand years ago, the exaggerations of the story tellers over the previous millennia had morphed these human heroes into powerful gods who enlivened their endless lives by creating humans as their toys.

Years later all this research paid off. As an untrained teacher, at the mercy of an unruly class of fifteen-year old miscreants, many with police records, I resorted to Scheherazade's life-saving tactic.

'Listen! Listen!' I shouted, 'and I'll tell you a story.'

Gradually the sneering, mocking, merciless lads began to simmer down and listen.

'Shut up! Shut up! I can't hear the story,' yelled the ringleader, soon to go off to borstal.

The blood and guts Viking saga had found kindred spirits. The monster had just torn the hind leg off a horse and was about to bash the hero's head in with it when the end of lesson bell rang.

'Oh, what a shame!' said I, who had deliberately slowed the story down to run over time. 'I'll have to finish the story next lesson.'

The ruffians stormed in next lesson demanding the rest of the story.

'Can't take up another whole lesson with a story: I'll get the sack. Tell you what: we could get the work done very fast to make time at the end for the story.'

I watched, amazed, as they worked hard to complete the exercise. When I'd finished the story I asked if they would like another at the end of the next lesson.

'There's more stories like that?'

'You bet,' said I. 'Some are even bloodier, and I've got a million of 'em.'

I enjoyed telling stories as much as they enjoyed listening, so teaching became quite exciting and fun.

After ten years of teaching, my biggest audience ballooned to more than eight hundred, and blood and guts were no longer appropriate. My stories needed a sober moral purpose. I found books of homilies for assemblies and congregations but they seemed alien to me. In desperation I composed a fifteen minute story in the car whilst driving to and from the school. It went down very well. I gave away the books of homilies and happily composed two stories a week for the next five years. Crawling along in traffic jams was no longer irksome. For obvious reasons I couldn't write them down, so, as I rehearsed them, they were never exactly the same twice over. I came to believe that this spontaneity was essential to fully engage an audience.

Finally, as a Headteacher, I decided to perform only once a week to give my senior staff the other four days to practise the art of engaging large audiences. I no longer had to commute, so usually composed my weekly story relaxing in the bath.

When no one wanted to study Latin to O Level, I had to dismiss the teacher. The most vocal parents saw Latin as a status symbol, and demanded it should be taught to someone in the school. I offered an optional lesson as an alternative to a games lesson. Eight pupils signed up because their parents insisted. Another eight were prepared to do anything to get out of games lessons (He! He!) By Christmas word had got around about the stories from ancient Greek and Roman literature and the class had grown from sixteen to 43. They were sitting on the window ledges. Great fun. Yes, we did do some useful Latin as well.

Early retirement cost me my audience. My head is still seething with stories, more entertaining to me than anything on TV or in other people's books. What to do with them? Tell them to my computer. It seemed strange at first to see them written down instead of hearing myself tell them; strange to see them stay the same each time I look at them, and not vary, depending on the mood I'm in, or what I've just heard or witnessed.

Will anyone else want to read my stories? I realise my interests are a little eccentric. Lacking a family I doubt I could write a credible modern family saga. Revisiting my own childhood is unpleasant, and so were the stories told me by my disadvantaged pupils. Heads don't hear much about the home life of the happy families.

After fifty-five years of very happy marriage to my best pal, my husband, I've no patience with self-inflicted woes like love triangles, power struggles, selfish posturing, or petty trouble-making.

My novels are a little different. The leading characters are trying to pass as normal humans, which is growing ever more difficult with each new surveillance technique that is invented. Who or what are they?

Goodness Knows!

910 Words

TASK: Write a final chapter of your autobiography.

THE FINAL CHAPTER

'The trouble with writing your autobiography,' said my brother-in-law, 'is that it makes you look so self-obsessed.' He's just finished his: A4 sized, full of interesting pictures; no problems with the text – he's a computer whizz and has already published a book.

Self-obsessed? Look at the youngsters, arms out-stretched, blocking your way, filming themselves pulling faces at their smartphones, or clamping the phones to their ears and boring all their mates with their self-indulgent hang-ups! And look at the Daily Mail Wall of Shame! All those narcissists, flaunting acres of bare boobs, bums and torsos and trout-pouting at the camera!

Pretend you're applying for a job, or the Next World. You'd lay out your stall, display all your talents and experience. You wouldn't consider that to be narcissistic. (Imagine what Narcissus would have done with a smart phone. He'd be under a bus in no time, wouldn't he?)

'The trouble with retirement,' said a former teacher, 'is that I've a head packed with knowledge that's taken me a lifetime to acquire, but now I've no use for it at all.'

That's the trouble with age: gradually (or suddenly) it robs you of the chance to use the skills you've spent a lifetime learning. What use are the ten languages, ancient and modern, I've studied? I could tap dance once, and shoot a can off a wall. Yea, Yea! Youngsters don't believe you, or they think things must have been much easier in the old days. They weren't. Before the days of Health and Safety the world was a much more dangerous place. If you came a cropper it was more fool you, not somebody's fault for not removing the hazard. You fragile little Snowflakes don't know you're born.

While reading other people's autobiographies we are looking into their lives from the outside. Now we are on the inside, looking out, waiting for the shutters to crash down for the last time, and stay down forever. The more we have already done with our lives, the harder it gets to find something new to pass whatever time is left.

As my husband lay dying I asked how he rated his life, expecting sad complaints, as twenty-five years of Parkinson's Disease had blinded and paralysed him .

'Think where we started,' he said. 'It's been fantastic, amazing, far better than anything I ever dreamed of when I was growing up in the slums.'

His ashes are now behind a seat with both our names on on the promenade. He'd like that. He loved the sea and we were best pals for fifty-five years. He packed so much into life: was an officer in the RAF, then a Director of a big international company. He had all the trappings: huge office, big Merc, beautiful secretary, chauffeur on tap, turned left on planes and stayed in the best hotels. He ran a branch of the company in Johannesburg for a while and we drove and flew from one end of Africa to another. When he visited the branches in India we were welcomed like royalty. For two kids from the slums it was mind blowing.

He was made redundant by his heartless employers when they discovered he was ill, then he worked till he could hardly stand up as a consultant.

Luckily the illness struck when we had already skied down most of the black runs in the Alps, including La Sache and Face de Bellevarde. the Olympic Downhill course. We had sailed solo catamarans and an Americas Cup winner. We had skied off the top of a mountain to sail up into the sky hanging from a hang glider, and we had parachuted into the sea.

As he deteriorated I took early retirement to take him around the world. It was a wrench to leave the job I had loved for sixteen years, Headteacher of an idyllic comprehensive in twenty seven acres of gorgeous grounds. It had felt like a reward for my years in some pretty tough inner city schools.

Of course we went around the Horn, but not under sail. It was flat as a millpond. He was fascinated by the strangeness of Japan and Nepal, and the friendliness of the Chinese. We loved Hong Kong, spent two weeks there saying goodbye, good luck, when it was about to be handed back to the Chinese.

We loved Australia, spent about ten weeks exploring it end to end, ditto New Zealand – a beautiful country where the geological processes happen in full view.

We house-hunted down both sides of the USA, then chose Spain instead, for it's well-preserved medieval cities and lively little towns, spending the winters in lovely ancient Marbella, with its Arab remains.

I'm a workaholic, adrift without my comprehensive school to run, which had offered a crisis a minute, so life was never quiet or dull. With nothing to do except feed Mike his pills, I began giving lectures on Art, Architecture and Classical Music. I must have given far more than five hundred altogether, along the south coast of Spain in winter and of England in the Summer. I fell in love with many of the paintings I was showing, bought oils and canvases and painted copies to decorate our flats. My pride and joy is Michelangelo's Sybil, from the Sistine Chapel ceiling. She took me thirty hours to paint.

Mike liked a lot of space around him. With him gone our two homes seemed frighteningly empty. I sold them both in days. Buy very carefully: sell in a flash. I now have a cosy flat in a community where things are happening all the time. As usual I designed furniture as well as the décor for my new solo home. I've been Chairman of the Board here, among other things.

I've settled in Bournemouth because it is a beautiful leafy resort buzzing with life. Its University and language schools attract hordes of lively young people from all over the World. It's also the home of 'The World's Favourite Orchestra,' the BSO, now celebrating its 125th Birthday. Ambitious from the start, they made the first orchestral recordings in Britain, hosted all the famous conductors and invited composers from across Europe to conduct their own work.

I've become an enthusiastic patron. They took me to Hamburg to help choose a new concert grand, and to hear them play in the Ballroom of Buckingham Palace, invited by Princess Alexandra.

Domesticity is not my thing. I need something thrilling to think about. I've done life in the slums - got the T-shirt. My novels show a glamorous world where exciting opportunities are the norm. I do as many of the stunts I describe as I can, then push the imagined action a bit further, beyond most people's capabilities.

I wish I had wings. A few years ago I began flying a microlight, with a former fighter pilot as instructor, then went on to small planes and a helicopter. Imagine the thrill of landing your plane on the runway at RAF Kemble, former home of the Red Arrows, and then following a Typhoon Eurofighter down onto Bournemouth's runway. I really did those things, just after our annual airshow.

So, what devilment can I get up to now? Singapore for Book 3? My novels star a group of people who can't stay dead. Do I envy them? No. We were lucky to inhabit an era and a country where life was relatively safe and full of opportunities. The world is a cruel place.

Will I ever get to Book 6? Why Not! That's its title,

'Goodness Knows Why Not!'

1273 words

CREATING A BOOK COVER

Matt finish book covers seem to be the latest fashion, but smart, shiny, wear-clean ones cost no more.

The 13 by 19.6 novel can be covered by a single sheet of A4 paper: back, spine and front all one continuous picture, with a little overlap all around for leeway. You will need to find a picture. You could adapt one of the free ones from the internet, or better still, one of your own photographs, enlarged to A4 sideways (landscape) size. I painted my own once, having failed to find an existing one I liked. Try to make the spine look interesting. It is all you can see when the book is in the bookshelf. Set out the words for the front and back covers on separate 13 by 19.6 pages. The printing company can fuse the wording onto the cover picture and the spine as well.

It is normal to put only the title and author on the front and spine, and to write an advert for your work on the back. That 'blurb' should be as short as possible, so anyone seeking something to buy can take it in quickly. Use a big typeface so people can read it easily. Leave space at the bottom left for the ISBN stamp if you want to register your work with Nielsen's and the British Library. Your printers may be able to advise you how to do that.

You may see no easy way to sell your work at present but why not make sure it is all ready to go if a chance occurs in the future.

FINAL JOBS

On the flyleaf of your book you should state you are the author and claim copyright over it. If it is a novel you can assert that all the characters are pure invention.

If the work is an autobiography you could issue an apology in advance to anyone who feels in any way insulted by it. You may like to dedicate it to someone.

Look at the fly leaves of a few novels to see how this is normally done. It can be interesting to see how many different companies have had a hand in turning each of those works into books. No wonder the professionals take so long about it. All those people, all that work! We have done nearly all of that ourselves, all on our own.

You may want to create a contents list, but then you will have to think up titles for your chapters. I can see little point in labelling them only chapter 1, chapter 2. etc. Now, if it said: 'Chapter 10: Uncle Clifford Plays for Yorkshire.' 'Chapter 11: Uncle Clifford's Murder' there would be some point in a contents list.

SELLING YOUR WORK

Since you have spent so little money creating your book you might like to waste a little trying to sell a few copies. There are firms that specialise in marketing books. Some charge writers only a few hundred pounds. You may not get your money back but you wont have lost much and it might be fun. You'd need to be pretty fit and enterprising: they expect you to do most of the work yourself, following their advice. You may be sent to bookshops and literary festivals, hoping to sign copies of your work. At a local festival recently I saw no one buy a book written by any of the authors who were present.

If your book can be linked to a lecture you could try public speaking. Some organisations pay quite a lot to their speakers, and you might sell a book or two.

Amazon is a popular marketplace for self-published books. It is free to set up the mechanisms to sell downloads or printed books on demand but complicated. There are web sites on the Internet explaining the procedures, and organisations offering to do it for you.

If you don't care about the money you could chase fame. Social media are the route to fame these days, so if you can make your website famous, raise enough interest in thousands of people prepared to accept a free copy of your work, you might win the title of most downloaded work on Kindle. Many authors are giving away cartloads of free books as downloads, and even printed novels are on sale for as little as 99p. It's hard to understand the economics of that, given the cost of printing and paper.

But we are not in this to make money, are we? We write because we enjoy it, and to prove to ourselves that we have the determination and skill to create a competent finished product.

We are not trying to please the critics. We are not trying to write to a formula to sell our work. We are entertaining ourselves, creating imaginary worlds run by our rules or reliving the highlights of our lives. Writing inspires us to research new things and it's good mental exercise. For many of us this second life we can live in our minds and our books is more fun than the real one.

Now, is your book sitting on your bookshelf? Maybe it soon will be. The very best of luck with all your writing.

GOODNESS KNOWS WHAT!

Book 1

Justin Chase expects 'innocent young' Lucrezia to be easy prey when he takes her home to his glamorous Rome penthouse, a cool haven in the scorching heat of August. He is in for a big surprise. It may cost him his life.

A black comedy with something for everyone: sex and supercars, music, dancing, war planes, Ancient Rome, Renaissance Italy, fire, torture, cooking, art - you name it, it's probably here.

The first instalment of the adventures of a group of 'unusual' people. Who or WHAT are they?

By Jay Lumb

GOODNESS KNOWS HOW!

Book 2

In the second instalment of this entertaining black comedy we meet more of the lethally adventurous Monrosso family, who seem likely to lose their idyllic but bankrupt estate beside Lake Como.

Justin Chase dusts off his computer-hacking skills, but their amusing efforts to reduce their debts are not enough. Bounty hunting seems their only hope. Behind each other's backs, Cesare and Lucrezia each return to the Middle East war zones, with shocking consequences.